Autohypnosis for Franz Bardon´s

Initiation into Hermetics

by

Ray del Sole

Autohypnosis for Franz Bardon´s

Initiation into Hermetics

Copyright © by Ray del Sole, 2012

ISBN: 978-1-291-02361-9

All rights reserved including the right to reproduce this work in any form whatsoever, without permission in writing from the author, except for brief passages in connection with a review.

Art work: Copyright © by Ray del Sole, 2012
Front cover: Photo: Karl-Ludwig G. Poggemann, „ look downstairs into stairwell whirl ", CC-Lizenz (BY 2.0)
Back cover: Photo: Bonsai, „Nur ein Sonnenuntergang", CC-Lizenz (BY 2.0)
http://creativecommons.org/licenses/by/2.0/de/deed.de
Source: www.piqs.de

Attention

Please regard that you take the responsibility for all exercises, experiments and advices you do or follow in this book. All warnings of spiritual teachers, especially by Franz Bardon, Indian Yogis and me should be taken serious. Spiritual training is an art and science and not something to play with or for curiosity. Spiritual development takes years, whole life times, many incarnations indeed. As you are an eternal being you have time enough to proceed step by step keeping the balance in all aspects.

With respect to the law of perfection we combine the male principle of will with the female principle of subconsciousness so that the magical development unfolds in its best way. We sow the seeds of new qualities, abilities and powers into the fertile field of our subconsciousness and let the transformation begin.

Ray del Sole

I dedicate this work to all true seekers of the eternal light. May it serve your development to real mastership.

Ray del Sole

TABLE OF CONTENTS

INTRODUCTION	14
Hypnosis – what you should regard	**16**
DISCLAIMER OF LIABILITY FOR SELF-HYPNOSIS INSTRUCTIONS	16
CONTRAINDICATIONS FOR HYPNOSIS	16
COMPLICATING FACTORS FOR HYPNOSIS	17
Theory	**18**
THE POLARITY OF MIND	18
INTELLIGENCE, AWARENESS AND CONSCIOUSNESS	19
AUTOSUGGESTION VERSUS AUTOHYPNOSIS	21
RESULT AND PROGRESS IMAGINATION	23
AUTOHYPNOSIS EXAMPLE: DISSOLVING OF BLOCKADES	26
Practice	**28**
THE RIGHT PREPARATION FOR AUTOHYPNOSIS	28
INDUCTION	31
PROGRAMMING THE MUDRA	33
THE PLACE TO BE	33
LEAD OUT	35
THE PIKA-PIKA-BREATHING	36
Autohypnosis for Bardon´s ten steps	**37**

FIRST STEP - SUGGESTIONS ... 37
Summary of exercises of step I: ... 37
Magic mental training (I) – suggestions ... 38
Magic psychic training (I) – suggestions ... 40
Magic physical training (I) – suggestions ... 41

SECOND STEP - SUGGESTIONS ... 44
Summary of exercises of step II: ... 44
Magic mental training (II) – suggestions ... 45
Magic psychic training (II) – suggestions ... 48
Magic physical training (II) – suggestions ... 49

THIRD STEP - SUGGESTIONS ... 51
Summary of exercises of step III ... 51
Magic mental training (III) – suggestions ... 52
Magic psychic training (III) – suggestions ... 53
Magic physical training (III) – suggestions ... 54

FORTH STEP - SUGGESTIONS ... 57
Summary of exercises of step IV ... 57
Magic mental training (IV) – suggestions ... 58
Magic psychic training (IV) – suggestions ... 59
Magical physical training (IV) – suggestions ... 61

FIFTH STEP - SUGGESTIONS	63
Summary of exercises of step V	*63*
Magic mental training (V) – suggestions	*64*
Magic psychic training (V) – suggestions	*65*
Magical physical training (V) – suggestions	*66*
SIXTH STEP - SUGGESTIONS	69
Summary of exercises of step VI	*69*
Magic mental training (VI) – suggestions	*70*
Magic psychic training (VI) – suggestions	*72*
Magic physical training (VI) – suggestions	*73*
SEVENTH STEP - SUGGESTIONS	73
Summary of exercises of step VII	*73*
Magic mental training (VII) – suggestions	*74*
Magic psychic training (VII) – suggestions	*74*
EIGHTH STEP - SUGGESTIONS	76
Summary of exercises of step VIII	*76*
Magic mental training (VIII) – suggestions	*77*
Magic psychic training (VIII) – suggestions	*78*
Magic physical training (VIII) – suggestions	*81*
NINTH STEP - SUGGESTIONS	82

Summary of exercises of step IX	*82*
Magic mental training (IX) – suggestions	*83*
Magic psychic training (IX) – suggestions	*83*
Magic physical training (IX) – suggestions	*85*
TENTH STEP - SUGGESTIONS	85
Summary of exercises of step X	*85*
Magic mental training (X) – suggestions	*86*
Magic psychic training (X) – suggestions	*87*
Magic physical training (X) – suggestions	*88*
Additional applications	**90**
THE RIGHT ATTITUDE	90
MEETING YOUR SPIRITUAL GUIDE	91
CLEARING AND HEALING	91
CLEARING AND HEALING OF OLD KARMA	93
PSYCHIC HYGIENE	95
MASTERSHIP	96
IMMUNE SYSTEM	97
CHARISMA	98
SELF-RESPECT / SELF-CONFIDENCE	99
THE RIVER OF LIFE	101

Motivation	102
Superlearning	104
Epilogue	**107**
Contact	**108**
Index	**110**

Introduction

Dear student of Bardon´s "Initiation into Hermetics",

just like you I follow the holy path towards the aim of human evolution. The path is very long and really rocky. Dangers and traps are waiting for the careless traveler. And sometimes obstacles appear which seem to be insurmountable. Then you are forced to stop on your way. You look at the obstacle and start to think about all the sacrifices, the hard work and training but also about the great experiences you already had in the past on your spiritual adventure trip. "Was all the effort for nothing? Am I supposed to stop my journey here?" Such thoughts might appear in your mind while examining the barrier in front of you. And now, what are you going to do? Do you give up or do you try everything to overcome it?

I have been traveling the holy path already for a long time and so I know all difficulties and problems. The training of Bardon is more than demanding. It is like climbing the Mount Everest without any preparation, - an understatement to say that this is extreme. And indeed you must be extreme to master the direct path.

On the other hand we are dealing here with magic. Magic has secret aspects in the same way like Bardon´s books and teachings. So when you understand the secrets of magic and when you can read between the lines in his books then you can perform wonders, - wonders of progress where progress seems to be impossible.

One big and important secret for progress on the path is the smart use of the power of the subconsciousness. Most students do not understand the importance of the subconsciousness and they also do not understand the relation of will and subconsciousness. Bardon gave only a few hints about it.

In the following I will describe the secret relation between them and how the subconsciousness is used in best way for progress on the path.

I hope and wish to serve you with this book in your spiritual development so that you become a real temple of the divine spirit like it is foreseen for all of us.

Certainly only those students with the right attitude can count on full success. For all others Divine Providence will find a way to distract them from the path (for their own security).

Ray del Sole

Hypnosis – What You Should Regard

Disclaimer of Liability for Self-Hypnosis Instructions

All techniques, suggestions and instructions are proved and regard the latest professional standard of hypnosis applications. Nevertheless you use the following instructions for autohypnosis at your own risk and responsibility. I like to point out that I do not assume any liability, especially for own suggestions, which lead to physical or psychological damage or other disadvantages that have arisen from the application of self-hypnosis. Please regard the contraindications!

Contraindications for Hypnosis

If you are not in good health than please consult your doctor. Ask him if there are any risks for you in using self-hypnosis.

In the following cases hypnosis should not be applied:

- For mentally handicapped people (because the brain functions are impaired and the effect of hypnosis is difficult to foresee)
- People with heavy heart and circulatory diseases in which deep relaxation is contraindicated, such as heart failure
- For psychosis (schizophrenia, bipolar disorder, dysthymia, borderline personality disorders or other serious mental illnesses, especially if there are delusional or dissociative symptoms)
- Depression in general (some hypnosis techniques can actually intensify depression)
- In the case of alcohol or drug abuse

- For personality disorders (hypnosis is here only little or not at all successful)
- For people who had just recently (last week) a heart attack or stroke
- For people with addictions like alcohol, drugs or pain medication dependence - Smokers are here except of course
- For patients with thrombosis (risk that the clot is in motion and raises an embolism)

COMPLICATING FACTORS FOR HYPNOSIS

The following factors can make it complicate to come into trance and reach good results:

- Migraine (with filtering problems in the brain, the client is phased or permanently hypersensitive e.g. against noise and the brain may have problems to leave the waking state).
- ADD / ADHD (in this disorder, the brain has problems to produce certain frequencies, thus it is possible that the brain cannot reach the hypnotic state).
- Severe fatigue / tiredness of the student (the body tends to relax and fall asleep so that the brain can only maintain a limited hypnotic state).
- Low blood pressure - people with low blood pressure often have an increased tendency to fall asleep. After the hypnosis the student needs enough time to be fully awake again before he does something like driving a car.
- Hormonal disorders such as thyroid disease and related medication, hormonal imbalances caused by menopause, etc.

Theory

The polarity of mind

In the chapter about autosuggestion Bardon gives first explanations about the negative aspect of the subconsciousness and how the subconsciousness can be used in a positive way for training. As usual Bardon leaves it up to the student to discover further secrets by real practice. At this point I do not want to describe all aspects of mind but only the few which are important for this book.

The human mind consists of a very interesting polarity. There is a male pole and a female pole:

Male pole:

- Ajna Chakra (center)
- Fire element
- Normal consciousness
- Active
- Fertilizing function

Female pole:

- Back head chakra (center)
- Water element
- Subconsciousness
- Passive
- Parturient function

In an ideal way both poles work together as a unit in harmony. The male pole fertilize the female pole with ideas, thoughts and wishes and the female pole gets pregnant and gives birth to them. In different words the subconsciousness helps to manifest ideas and wishes in its female function.

If the relation between both poles is in imbalance then we experience similar problems like in a marriage where the love is somehow gone and the unit is broken. Then there is stress between both poles and real disharmony. The poles work against each other. Bardon speaks about this effect.

Today many people and also spiritual students have problems with this polarity of mind in form of negative thoughts like doubts, fears and lacking of self-confidence. Then there is the problem that students have often a major focus on the principle of will, the active pole, in the training and that they forget to use the female principle in the same way. This is certainly unlawful as both poles have to work together to create new qualities, abilities and powers. To understand this right please think about how a baby is brought to life. The man makes the woman pregnant. This takes an amount of sperms and some action. But the woman is pregnant with the baby for nine whole months. You see the difference? The male pole sows a single seed and the female part cares for the nourishment and growing of this seed. In different words the female pole has a major function in the realization of an idea. And now you understand the importance of the use of the subconsciousness for the training. Without the conscious use of the female nourishing and materialization quality and power not much progress can be gained.

INTELLIGENCE, AWARENESS AND CONSCIOUSNESS

I have spoken already about normal consciousness as one pole and the so called subconsciousness as the other pole. The polarity here is reflected by the Ajna chakra and the back head chakra. Beside this central polarity of mind we have many centers of consciousness, - the Indian chakras. Meanwhile scientists have discovered that there are agglomerations of neural cells which are located at the points of the chakras. These neural centers work indeed like small brains and have a kind of consciousness and intelligence. So indeed intelligence and consciousness is not limited to the brain but can be found in bigger and smaller centers in the whole body. The old initiates knew this long time ago already but today it is rediscovered. Here we can follow the old knowledge about the chakras and the scientific research on them from Choa Kok Sui, the founder of Pranic Healing. In general we can observe that the chakras contain all degrees of intelligence, perception and feelings from divine over human down to animalistic levels. The power and quality of these centers depend on the individual degree of development. In conclusion we can say that the human personality is "spread" in the whole body or better microcosm. The different centers or chakras are points to access the different aspects of personality. All centers are interdependent, in interaction, a network. Again here reflects the microcosm the macrocosm, the spheres. Besides these centers of consciousness we can say that all organs and all cells have a kind of intelligence, spirit and awareness. In fact spirit, intelligence, awareness can be found everywhere in the whole micro- and macrocosm. So when we work with the subconsciousness then many different forms of intelligence are involved. One might think that hypnotic or auto hypnotic treatment is limited to the human individual, to the microcosm. This is not the case as a human being is interdependent and networked with creation. So indeed other beings which hear your suggestions or which witness your treatment can take part and work on you for clearing, healing, development, etc. Last but not least your spiritual guide can monitor and influence the treatment. So we deal indeed with the own conscious ideas, own subconscious work and help from outside of our microcosm.

Autosuggestion versus Autohypnosis

Bardon recommends autosuggestion as a technique to work with the subconsciousness. For this technique a state of relaxation or a "near to sleep" state is suggested. Then you repeat your autosuggestion a longer time either until you fall into sleep when you do it in bed in the late evening or until you have reached the set amount of beads. So indeed autosuggestion has its focus in the bigger number of repetitions of one single autosuggestive sentence. The repetition of an idea respectively of the sentence has a strengthening effect which makes the idea growing, - materializing. It is similar to sow a seed into the earth (subconsciousness) and to water it each day so that it can grow to a plant. After a longer time of training autosuggestion exercises lead automatically into deeper states of mind as repetition is somehow dull and lets the normal consciousness "shut down". Therefore repetition is already a way of changing the state of mind, a way of hypnosis. Hypnosis can be defined as a state of mind where the subconsciousness is receptive while the normal consciousness is "shut down". Normal consciousness means here especially the male part of the mind, - will, intellect, the active, questioning, defending part. This is important as only the subconsciousness does not differentiate between reality and imagination / suggestions. In contrary the normal consciousness differentiates and works like a guard and defender of mind, cognition and personality. The normal consciousness does not accept all ideas, also not all good ideas for positive changes. So a shift towards the subconsciousness is necessary to make self-influence work.

With these explanations we come to autohypnosis which is indeed not far away from autosuggestion. It is nearly the same and trained autosuggestion becomes autohypnosis automatically. Certainly you can start directly with autohypnosis as a deeper and more effective form of autosuggestion. The only and main difference here is that you start your exercise with suggesting yourself that you become more and more relaxed and that you enter a deeper and deeper state of relaxation and trance. When you have reached a very deep state of mind, - trance, relaxation then you start with your original, actual suggestion. A small spot of normal consciousness is kept by which gives these suggestions to the subconsciousness. In this deep state it is also not necessary to create one sentence which you repeat (but you can do so). In contrary you can "talk to yourself" like you know it from hypnotists talking to their clients. It can be like a meditation upon a new ability for example where you think about how this ability manifests, how you use it, how great it is, how it becomes stronger and stronger, how it refines itself, etc. These ideas and images are directly received by your subconsciousness and your subconsciousness takes them for real and acts like this. In this way the new ability realizes thanks to your subconsciousness. (The other part is certainly the real and conscious training of the wished for reality. Both aspects – male and female have to go hand in hand for best results in time.) After the part of "talking to yourself/ meditation/ autosuggestion you have to lead yourself back into normal consciousness. This means that you have to come back from your deep state of relaxation and trance into the state of normal activity. You give yourself the command to increase blood pressure and breathing to a normal level, then that you feel fresh and awake and at last you open your eyes completely refreshed, fully awake, right here and right now. This is useful and important to really switch from trance to normal activity. A half-trance in everyday life is not good and can be dangerous (think of driving a car for example).

As you can see autosuggestion and autohypnosis are quite simple techniques which provide real success in the work on yourself. Everyone with a normal condition of health can use them. For autohypnosis there exist further techniques where you use so-called triggers, anchors, special codes or rituals to combine whished for states of consciousness or abilities with an external sign to start or use them directly. Such things we know from all religions and traditions where rituals have been used to induce special states of mind and soul. Today such triggers are set for a quick access to the trance state and also to recall a special psychic setting for high performance in sports for example. But as Bardon describes it you can build your own rituals, etc. for all purposes just as you like.

RESULT AND PROGRESS IMAGINATION

In hypnotherapy there is a technique where you go back into your past to experience important situations again to solve problems in the presence. It is called regression. It is possible that you feel and act like a child in such a session like you did in the past where you have gone under hypnosis. Something similar is possible with your future. It is called progression. Set into your own future you experience yourself much older and maybe wiser as your future-self. It is possible that you say what happened in the last years as a review. The point is that you have changed in your character and that maybe new abilities or qualities are there – just because you are older. Imagine that you are in a long term martial arts training. Due to the hypnosis session you experience yourself ten years older. So now you are no longer a beginner in martial arts but an old grand master. This is a different experience, a different feeling and attitude. With such a progression technique you can connect from your presence to energies and experiences of your future. You know how it feels like to be a master and this already as a beginner. Besides a real progression into your own future you can use imagination to experience yourself as a master, - a master in magic, an enlightened, refined and powerful being. Just get into meditation and ask yourself: "How do I experience myself as a master? How does it feel like to be one?" The chances are good that you indeed get to know such a state, the qualities, the attitude of a master, maybe you get into contact with according spiritual powers and maybe you have impressions about how it is to have new abilities. With such impressions it is easier for you to focus on your spiritual development as you know what is waiting for you.

Beside these more general things there is one technique which I suggest to you for a better progress in developing abilities/qualities. It could be named "Creating the Master":

Your aim is to reach complete mastership in magic and mystic. This is the basis. One part of the technique is "result imagination" and the other part is "process imagination" (simulation). Bardon suggests to imagine yourself having already reached your aim, - the wished for state. This is "result imagination". With this technique you vitalize the desired idea, image with mental energy and with emotional energy so that it manifests from the highest plane down to the material world. This can take a while and has to be repeated like watering a flower. "Process imagination" or simulation is the second part. Here you simulate in your imagination the wished for ability, quality/behavior or state in process of training/using. Indeed you create a new reality which supports the manifestation of your wish. We can say that it is a reality for your subconsciousness as it does not differentiate between imagination and "real" reality. In other words your imagined reality is real but on a different plane. Let´s take an example:

Clairvoyance

a)   Result imagination:

I am clairvoyant. I can see with my third eye everything I wish to see on akashic, mental, astral and material plane over time and space. There are no limitations for my third eye. My third eye is in perfect condition, well trained and brilliant in its perception. My view is clear and all-permeating. I witness the wonders of creation. I can see the dwellers of the different realms, the beings of the elements, the gods and goddesses, the beings of nature, the flows of energy. I can see everything. I see the spiritual guides, the masters, the old prophets, the brothers and sisters in the light. I witness the history of mankind and the future. I discover the secrets of the pyramids, of old temples and ruins. All mysteries are open now for my third eye. I am omniscient like my father (God). I am a master of magic and mysticism. It feels great. I am blessed. I am thankful. I am a son (daughter) of God. And so on…

b)   Process imagination:

I am sitting in my asana, in a deep meditation state. I am not clairvoyant so far but I simulate it to create the desired reality which helps my subconsciousness to manifest it. Imagination: I focus on my third eye and feel that it is active and completely developed. My intention to see with my third eye is already enough to activate the sense of clairvoyance. I feel how my third eye and my throat chakra become more active. My consciousness has a slight shift and I see my own aura with its colors. I focus now on the chakras. I see my active crown chakra and the inner chakra. I see the golden and violet colors. I see how the divine energy enters my head, my energy system and how it flows through my nadis. I can see the big chakras but also the smaller ones. I can see into my body, the energy of my organs...I have watched my whole microcosm. How fascinating it is. I am thankful and happy for this brilliant ability. My clairvoyance gets better and better each day of training. Now I return to my normal sight and I finish the meditation. And so on…

This was just a small example. The more creativity, fantasy you put into your imaginations the better you nourish your desired reality. Most important is that you take part in these meditations with 100% - live it! Integrate all your senses and your emotions to make it real, to vitalize it. See yourself, feel yourself, experience yourself in the desired state. When you combine both parts – result and process imagination and repeat it regularly then you do the best to manifest what you wish for. As a third part real active training is certainly necessary. You can compare this with the training of a weightlifter. Imagination is important but real training is certainly necessary. Magical abilities need training similar to muscles. Structure has to be built.

You can be sure that all necessary ideas and energies exist already somewhere in creation for your new abilities and that you connect to them by such a training. During your magical training you can put step by step new abilities and qualities to your vision of mastership and so you complete yourself, your image until you and your perfect state are one.

AUTOHYPNOSIS EXAMPLE: DISSOLVING OF BLOCKADES

To give you a first good impression how autohypnosis works I present here a good technique to clear your blockades. Nearly all humans and also nearly all students suffer from different kinds of blockades which appear on all planes, - on the mental, astral and physical plane. Blockades appear especially in the energy channels, the nadis or meridians and also in the chakras which work as energy pumps, processing energy suppliers and distributors. Blockades are in main dirty, ill and slimy energies which adhere and clog the energy channels and chakras. Blockades can also be negative thought patterns and negative emotional patterns. On the physical plane there can be structures which block the flow of metabolism. When there is somewhere a blockade then there are parts of the body/soul/mind which have too much energy (congestion) and there are parts which get not enough fresh energy (deficiency). The human microcosm is able to dissolve blockades by itself (in most cases) but it is necessary to lead the attention of the subconsciousness to the blockades. It is necessary to give the right impulse for self-clearing and self-healing processes. The reason for this is that the subconsciousness is very busy with "multitasking", with thousands of processes in the human body and with this its power is not focused on self-healing. Maybe the subconsciousness is focused on digestion or something else (while a lot of other processes are working parallel). So when you take consciously time for self-healing and dissolving of blockades then your subconsciousness gets the necessary impulse and focuses its attention and power on this subject. The good thing is that the subconsciousness knows exactly where the blockades and negative energies are. It also knows what to do to dissolve them. This is indeed a big advantage.

The technique itself is quite simple. Do it and observe what is happening on all three planes in your body in the next time (within three days). Certainly you can repeat the exercise. And certainly your subconsciousness and your body need time for this work, - give the process of clearing and healing enough time. It is possible that in a first exercise a good amount of blockades is cleared. In a second round further blockades are cleared and in a third round maybe the last problems are dissolved. This depends on your health and inner balance, - on your needs for clearing. Maybe all blockades are cleared already in a first exercise. It also depends on your abilities to get into a deep state of mind. It can be useful to repeat from time to time such an exercise as new problems can appear. Just follow your intuition as always.

The technique:

Get into your asana. Close your eyes. Now focus your attention on your breathing. Tell yourself (mentally) that with every exhalation you get "deeper and deeper" into a state of full relaxation, into a state of trance. Alternatively or additionally you can move with your mind from your feet through all body regions upwards to your head. Rest a short while in every body region and imagine or tell that the region is totally relaxed, warm and feeling well. With this you relax your whole body completely. After this deep relaxation and deepening of your trance you focus with your mind into the center of yourself respectively you set yourself into the Akasha point of your microcosm. Now tell your subconsciousness respectively imagine that all blockades on the mental plane, in your soul and in your body dissolve completely. Imagine that your subconsciousness starts a great process of self-clearing. Imagine how all blockades dissolve, vanish, break, how new, fresh energies flow and circulate, how your nadis are cleared, how your chakras start to work, start to participate in this great work of clearing, refreshing and healing, imagine how all bad energies dissolve and spit out of your chakras, how these energies are exhaled by your lungs, how your whole microcosm rebalances itself on all planes. Release all your blockades, release all bad thoughts, all bad emotions, all what hurts you. Imagine how all your wounds are healed, how you recover on all planes. Thank your subconsciousness for the good work. Tell it to go on until you are completely cleaned and healed. Then focus on the idea that you inhale fresh, healing energies which support your subconsciousness in its great work until you feel saturated with fresh, good energies. Then stay a while in observing the work in your body. Observe how you feel better and better. Then make the steps back into normal activity. Say to yourself that you count up to three and with the number three you open your eyes and you feel completely awake, refreshed, right here and right now. One – your breathing and your blood pressure increase to normal degrees. Two – you feel awake, refreshed, back into your physical body. Three – you open your eyes and you are back in the "normal" world – back from trance.

This is a very effective exercise with a lot of benefits for yourself. It helps in normal life, in health problems and in spiritual training. I wish and hope that this exercise is a true blessing for you. May it serve your progress!

PRACTICE

THE RIGHT PREPARATION FOR AUTOHYPNOSIS

In general take care that all sources of disturbance are disabled. This is your mobile phone, your normal telephone, your PC, electrical devices, pets and any kinds of dates, meetings, etc. These are just the normal things which you know from your meditations and training.

Then you have four options:

1. You take the script and consult a hypnotherapist to install the wished for suggestions into your subconsciousness. This is easy and professional but is not for free.
2. You read and understand the suggestion and reconstruct it in your mind during your autohypnosis. This is good, easy and useful. Maybe it takes some training to be able to create the suggestions fluently.

3. You record the suggestion as a MP3-file and listen to it via headphones or the speakers of your hi-fi system. This is easy and comfortable but not flexible. Normal meditation is not fixed but a floating process. Recorded suggestions are more a matter of autosuggestion and clearly defined parts of autohypnosis.
4. You record them and you underlay them with special hypnotic music or sounds. I recommend here the use of the software Neuro Programmer 3. It is a professional tool for autosuggestion and brainwave modeling for states of trance. The hypnotic sounds help you to enter quickly a deep state of trance for good effects.
5. It is possible that you let the hypnotic music play in the background while you do it like I have described it in the second point.

Which option you follow is a matter of trying it out but also a matter of being a beginner or a professional in autohypnosis. The aim has to be to do your autohypnosis without any help like you do meditation. So if you like then do some experiments and find your individual way which fits best to your needs.

Let´s go to the next points:

Just follow the instructions and give your subconsciousness about three days to set the new programming. This means don´t think about it and just let it realize. This means that you should not sabotage the work of your subconsciousness by mental discussions in your mind if it works or not.

When you set an anchor or trigger then train it, - use it often until it is an automatic mechanism. Anchors or triggers are rituals, symbols, gestures, objects which are connected to the wished for attitude, effect, ability, result, etc.

Certainly you can individualize the texts of suggestions. The presented texts are examples to show you how a suggestion can be created and what is important. You can also enhance them or add further details like you know it from programming energy (look up the descriptions of Bardon).

Your autohypnosis starts always with an induction which leads you into a state of deep trance. Then the main part comes with the suggestions and at last you are led out into the normal state of being awake. These are three parts. The induction and the lead out are always the same and will become a natural habit by training. The more you train them the easier, better and faster you get into the state of trance. Also the effects will be better and certainly you will return easily to your normal waking state. It is all a matter of training. Your normal meditations and all exercises of the Bardon training will become easier providing better results as it is all a matter of getting into a meditative trance. Trance allows you all kinds of magical operations and experiments as your senses and your mind is focused on the mental or astral plane, - withdrawn from the physical world.

The technique is absolutely safe for you. If any kind of worst case should occur then you would awake by yourself after a short time without any problems.

Please use always the "Induction" + one suggestion (topic) + the "lead out". I present here useful suggestions for all steps of Bardon's Initiation into Hermetics plus further useful texts for general purposes.

When the word "BREAK" occurs then it means that you interrupt your speech for a few moments so that you are able to follow the instruction in the trance state.

Please be aware that some things are a matter of minutes, others may take an hour for realization and the complex ones with high requirements for maturity may take weeks or months. So always take your time!

It is very interesting to examine the changes in yourself. You will experience that centers and areas according to your topic will become active, also that old bad emotions and thoughts may rise in your consciousness as signs of clearing and healing. You can also expect signs for new abilities and progress. Be open for interesting processes and effects.

INDUCTION

Use your normal asana or meditation position. Choose a position for your hands or for your fingers which expresses for you a meditative state of trance. This can be a traditional mudra from Buddhism or Hinduism. The simplest form is to lay your hands on your thighs. Then program yourself: "Every time I lay my hands on my thighs in this way I get automatically in my meditative trance state." With some repetitions of training this will become true. It will have a ritualistic character.

(You can use the first person perspective "I do…" or the second person perspective "You do…". This is individual and you decision. Both works. You can also speak in this way, like to a second person, to your subconsciousness "you go now….". Just choose what you feel comfortable with.)

"Take a comfortable sitting position and perform your mudra (hand/finger position). Keep your head straight and close your eyes. Now focus on your breathing. Observe how you inhale and how you exhale, - inhale and exhale. Take a deep natural breath and then exhale and every time you exhale you fall deeper and deeper in a wonderful state of pure relaxation. Inhale and exhale, inhale and exhale and observe how all stress is released automatically, how all tension is dissolved, how you fall deeper and deeper into a wonderful state of pure and absolute relaxation. And with every breath you go deeper and deeper into this great feeling of pure relaxation. Focus on this natural breathing and examine how the air fills your lungs, how fresh air vitalizes your whole body and how the consumed air is exhaled together with all stress and unimportant thoughts and feelings. You can release all tension, all what does not belong to your meditation. Release it all and enjoy the inner peace and harmony which fills your whole soul, your mind and body, more and more with every breath you take. Now feel into your feet. Feel into your feet and examine how relaxed they are. Feel the pleasant warmth in your feet, the relaxation, the ease. And now feel into your lower legs. Feel how the wave of relaxation, pleasant warmth and ease fills your lower legs completely. Examine how relaxed and comfortable your lower legs are. And the wave of pleasant warmth, ease and relaxation flows on into your thighs. Examine how your thighs are filled with ease, warmth and a wonderful relaxation. Your legs and feet are completely relaxed, pleasantly warm and full of ease. Now focus on your pelvis and examine how the wave of relaxation fills your whole pelvis, a wonderful relaxation and pleasant warmth is filling your whole pelvis and spreads into your belly. Focus on your belly and feel the wave of ease, pleasant warmth and relaxation spreading, floating into your whole belly. And the wave of relaxation flows on into your chest, into your whole torso, into your spine and back. Your whole body is floated by this wonderful wave of relaxation, ease and pleasant warmth. It is so great to feel this deep relaxation, this deep inner peace and harmony. And now feel into your arms, into your hands and feel also there how this great wave of relaxation, ease and pleasant warmth is floating and filling your upper arms, your forearms, your hands and fingers. Your arms and hands are completely relaxed. Now focus your attention on your shoulders and your neck and feel the wave of relaxation, ease and pleasant warmth spreading in your shoulders and in your neck. Feel how your shoulders and your neck become totally relaxed and warm. And now feel into your jaw, into your tongue, feel the warmth, ease and relaxation spreading all over your jaw, tongue and mouth. Now focus on your temples, on your eyes and eyelids. Feel the wave of relaxation, pleasant warmth and ease entering your temples, eyes and eyelids. Feel how they become totally relaxed. And now focus on your forehead and feel how it gets warm and relaxed, how all tension is vanishing. Focus on your whole head, on the skin of your head and let your whole head become pleasantly warm, easy and relaxed. Focus now again on your whole body and feel the deep and pleasant relaxation, peace and harmony in your whole body. It feels so good to release all tension, all stress, all unimportant thoughts and emotions. You feel fine and absolutely well. You are completely relaxed in a wonderful state of deep trance."

Programming the mudra

Train your mudra together with the induction and lead out several times until both feel natural and easy for you. Then continue with other suggestions. When you do the lead out then dissolve automatically your mudra! The mudra will be a great help for all exercises and meditations.

"Now focus on your mudra. The position of your hands and fingers has a special meaning. Whenever you put your hands and fingers in this special position you automatically enter a deep state of meditation, relaxation and trance. You automatically release all stress, all unwanted thoughts and emotions and you become ready for your meditation, for your mental and astral work. And every time when you dissolve your mudra you become automatically awake, feeling fresh and vital. The use of your mudra becomes natural for you, a habit which works automatically. You only have to perform your mudra and automatically you enter your state of meditation and trance. And every time you dissolve your mudra you enter automatically your normal waking state, feeling fresh and vitalized. This program is now anchored in your subconsciousness so that your mudra will work perfectly for you."

The place to be

In the physical reality you are sitting in a room of your flat or house for meditation. But this is not a must for the mental and astral reality. In fact it is up to you where you want to practice. First option: It doesn´t matter for you, so you do not think about it. Second option: You imagine yourself a place in nature where you meditate and do your exercises, a place you love, feel well and which is special for you. Maybe a place in a forest, on a rock, in the hills, on a holy mountain, on a meadow, at a lake or wherever. Third option: You imagine a holy temple for yourself where you meditate, practice and do your magical operations.

Certainly the choice is individually and up to you. If you use a special place in nature or a temple then this can enhance your training and work. It can help you to develop your senses, it can help you to create sacred spaces with special energetic atmospheres and it can be a place where you meet your spiritual guide, masters, brothers and also higher beings, etc. During your training you can enhance your place/temple with special rooms or further places for healing, clearing, for special abilities, for special meditations, for the use of special energies. It is all up to you. Indeed you create your reality on the mental and astral plane according to your needs and wishes.

If you want to create a place or temple then it is necessary to substantiate your ideas, to think about the details. Here it might help to remember places in nature and temples you have visited already or you have pictures of. When your vision with details is ready you can imagine yourself in this place/temple. Then you can use your imagination with all senses to realize it on the mental and astral plane. Imagination is the power of creation. It is your tool to realize your ideas. See your place, see the details, smell the air, feel the atmosphere, hear the sounds. Make it real. And every time you get into your meditation strengthen your place/temple with your senses, with imagination.

"You are now in the meditative state of trance. Your senses have been withdrawn from the material world and shifted to the higher planes, to the experience of the mental and astral realms. You are now in this higher world where your imagination has creative power, where you can build and create whatever you wish for. The energy follows your will. What you wish for will realize. You are not limited by time and space and so you can move everywhere you want, into any landscape and any time. A thought is enough and immediately you are there where you want to be. Go now to the place you wish for. Look around yourself. What can you see? What can you hear? What can you feel? What do you smell? Become aware of your surroundings. And now if you like create the space as you wish to. Use your imagination with all senses. Give your place, your space form, color, light, fragrance, atmosphere, feelings, characteristics, function and meaning. Take your time and use your senses, your imagination. And every time you enter the state of meditation you will automatically be in your favorite place. And you will enhance and strengthen your place with all your senses automatically."

Lead Out

Use it always at the end of your auto hypnotic work.

"It is time now to awake, to come back into your waking consciousness, into the room you are sitting for hypnosis. I count now from one to three and with every number I say, you feel more and more awake and refreshed and when I say three you can open your eyes. You will feel really good, fully awake and completely refreshed. One – concentrate on your breathing and take a deep breath. Feel how your breathing reaches a normal level. Your blood pressure regulates to a normal waking state too. You feel more and more awake and you breathe deeply in and out. Two – you feel your body intensively, you feel your arms, hands, your legs and feet, you feel how vitality is coming back into your physical body. Now stretch your body, make fists, rotate your feet. Regulate your breathing to normal degrees. Take a deep breath. Continue to move your body. Three – open your eyes. You are now fully awake, refreshed and vitalized. Give yourself a few minutes to come back to the physical realm."

THE PIKA-PIKA-BREATHING

There are a few good ways to get into a hypnotic state of trance for auto-hypnosis. One is the concentration on the breathing and the relaxation of the body. Another is the progressive muscle relaxation and a very special one is the so-called pika-pika-breathing.

It is a very simple and powerful exercise which is used for quick self-hypnosis, for total relaxation and to stop pain.

The technique is simple: You become aware of your breathing, - how you inhale and exhale. Then you imagine that every time you inhale with your lungs you inhale also with your head from above into your body. And every time you exhale with your lungs you exhale with your feet outwards from your body. This you repeat several times and you will experience that you go into a hypnotic trance state very quickly, a state of total relaxation where you do not feel pain (and cannot move).

It is the leading technique for quickest self-hypnosis, total relaxation and pain stopping.

The degree of trance is depending of the times you use this special breathing. A few breaths will bring you into a normal state of useful trance for autohypnosis. When you do more breathing then you go into the deepest possible state of relaxation and trance and then you are only able to relax and to recover. After a while you will return to the normal state automatically.

So if you like you can make some experiments with this special technique and you can use it instead of my suggested breathing induction.

Autohypnosis for Bardon's Ten Steps

Bardon presents a lot of exercises and aims to realize. It makes not always sense to use for every exercise or ability a hypnotic suggestion text. Sometimes it is useful to use a target imagination, sometimes a process and target imagination makes sense. You can certainly individualize and enhance the texts or neglect them if you do not need them. The use of the provided suggestions is completely up to you and no must. The texts here work well as examples and hints for your own practice.

First Step - Suggestions

Summary of exercises of Step I:

Magic Mental Training

1. Thought control,
2. Discipline of thoughts
3. Subordination of thoughts
   a. Control of thoughts twice a day from 1-10 minutes
   b. Suppression of certain thoughts. Holding onto a chosen thought. Provoking stillness of mind.
   c. Magical diarizing. Self-criticism. Planning of thought-trains for the day or the week ahead.

Magic Psychic Training

1. Introspection of Self-Knowledge
2. Making of the (Black & White) Mirrors of the Soul with respect to the elements, in three spheres of activity.

Magic Physical Training

1. Habituation to normal or reasonable mode of life.
2. Conscious Breathing
3. Conscious reception of Food (Eucharistic mystery)
4. Magic of Water

MAGIC MENTAL TRAINING (I) – SUGGESTIONS

OBSERVATION OF THOUGHTS

"I can observe the train of thoughts easily. Like a silent observer I follow the train of thoughts which is flowing through my mind. I understand and feel that I am awareness and that my thoughts are guests which come and go. It is interesting to be aware of the diversity of thoughts flowing through my mind. I can observe where they come from and why they appear. I can feel them coming and leaving my mind. I can observe how my mind, my intellect works with them, how one thought is followed by another one, how thoughts are analyzed and synthesized, how they are detailed and substantiated. It feels so easy and natural to watch my thoughts. The more I observe them the less they come into my mind. And the less they come the better I can observe them. It feels easy and natural for me to observe the thoughts flowing through my mind."

CONTROL OF THOUGHTS

"I am able to control my thoughts. I am able to determine the kind of thoughts which enter my mind. It feels natural for me to control which kind of thoughts I allow to enter my mind. I know that there are useful thoughts, thoughts which fit to the present situation I have to face and that there are thoughts which are not useful at all, which disturb my concentration, which sabotage me and my work. The good and useful thoughts I allow to enter my mind. All other thoughts I stop and keep them outside of my mind. I have always full control over the content of my mind. I choose consciously the right kind of thoughts for my present situation. Controlling of thoughts feels easy and natural for me. It is easy to keep unwanted thoughts out of my mind and to invite good and useful thoughts."

Full concentration

"Whatever I do I do it with full attention, with my full concentration. I can focus my awareness, my attention completely on the things which I am busy with, on the situation I experience presently. It feels easy and naturally for me to focus myself completely on the present situation and my present activity."

Concentration

"I can focus on every kind of thought or idea easily. My concentration is perfect and works without any disturbances or disruptions. My concentration is like a laser beam, - simply perfect and powerful. My concentration skills improve, strengthen and refine daily. It feels easy and natural for me to focus my attention on something and to keep it as long as I want to. I can concentrate myself perfectly on everything I wish to. My concentration is powerful and stable. My concentration works perfectly as long as I want and without any disturbances or disruptions."

Emptiness of mind

"I am able to cause and to keep emptiness of mind without any upcoming thoughts. The more I focus on the stillness of mind in my exercises the easier and better I reach this state. My ability to keep the stillness of mind grows day by day. It feels more and more easy and natural for me to cause and to keep the emptiness of mind. I am aware that the stillness of mind let me connect to the source of life, to Akasha, to the primordial spirit and so I open myself to God, to receive divine intuition, divine inspiration and divine guidance. I open myself to receive the divine spirit. I know that the stillness of mind makes me the perfect vessel for enlightenment like a crystal glass is perfect to receive a precious vine. I am ready to receive the divine spirit. I am ready to receive enlightenment. I am perfect in the stillness of mind. I can enter and keep the stillness of mind easily and naturally."

Magic Psychic Training (I) – Suggestions

Self-criticism

"I do self-analysis daily so that I raise my self-awareness and my self-knowledge. I do self-criticism daily to discover my faults and imbalances to refine myself successfully. I know how important it is to analyze myself daily, to become aware of my faults and imbalances. I know how precious it is to clear myself of bad characteristics and to refine my personality to a higher form of inner harmony and peace. It feels natural for me to reflect on my behavior, on my thoughts and emotions. It supports my self-awareness and my attention. It improves my life and my relationships. Self-criticism helps me to refine my personality and to get to know me deeply."

Soul mirror work
"I have deep insights in my mistakes, my habits, my desires, my drives and my characteristics. I have a good intuition which helps me to assign them to the four elements in my soul mirrors. My understanding of the four elements in relation to the human personality, to mind and soul, grows daily. Deeper and deeper I understand the principles of the four elements. I am thankful that I gain complete self-knowledge by my self-analysis and soul mirror work. I know all my bad characteristics and imbalances and I know all my good characteristics and harmonies."

Magic physical training (I) – suggestions

Temperance
"I know the great values of temperance and harmony in life. Balance is a divine virtue. Balance means health, inner peace and being centered. Day by day I integrate more and more temperance and harmony in my life. Harmony and temperance manifest more and more in all aspects of my life. I enjoy the inner balance, the good health, the inner peace. I feel centered in myself, centered in my life, centered in my soul. It is the attitude of the master, the attitude for success. Temperance and harmony enhance my life."

Physical training
"I like doing my physical training including the use of the soft brush for my skin, the washing with cold water and the morning gymnastics. It feels good for me to do it daily as it supports my health and fitness. I enjoy brushing my skin, washing myself with cool water. I enjoy the morning gymnastics. This all feels so natural and good for me. It is an integrated

habit which I keep my whole life. The physical training works fine for me and I love it."

THE MYSTERY OF BREATHING

"I inhale and I exhale in a natural and deep way. I inhale and exhale naturally with my chest and belly. While I keep my natural breathing I add my imagination. I impregnate the air with my wish, - a useful idea, thought or feeling. Indeed the air contains now my wish and I can inhale the impregnated air with my imagination. I inhale through my nose the fresh air together with my wish. It is so easy to combine the natural breathing with my imagination. By this magical breathing I inhale what I wish for and feed my mind and soul. The ideas, thoughts, and feelings flow with the fresh air into my lungs and with this they get into my bloodstream, into my whole body, mind and soul. It feels easy and natural for me to use my imagination to impregnate the air that I inhale to manifest my wishes in my personality."

EUCHARISTIC MYSTERY

"Like the air I can impregnate food and drinks with my wishes. It is just a matter of imagination and so it feels easy and natural for me to impregnate my meals and drinks with my wishes. I know that my food and drinks contain my wishes and that I do not only feed my physical body but also my mind and soul so that my wishes realize. I always eat and drink my impregnated food consciously. From day to day I feel more and more how I absorb my wish together with the food. I feel how my wish integrates itself in my personality and realizes. I really like to impregnate food and drinks and to consume them consciously as it is a magical ritual."

BLESSING OF FOOD

"I know that I can bless my food with my hands. I hold my hands above my meal or my drink and set myself into a spiritual mood, into a state of unity with God. I feel this wonderful connection. In this state I let the spiritual energies flow from my hands into my food. The energy follows my wish, my will and imagination. Energy follows always the intention. And so I feel how the spiritual energies are flowing into my food or drink. I know that I can add good wishes to this flow of energy so that they realize when I eat the food. Then I eat my meal consciously and I can feel the higher energy, the better taste of my food and I know that my wish will realize."

MAGIC OF WATER

"Every time I wash myself with cool water all my faults, bad characteristics, stress, etc. are absorbed by the magnetism of the water and washed away. Every time I wash my hands with cool water, the water absorbs all things I do not want, all bad energies, all stress, all imbalances, etc. Every time I use the shower I clean my body and I clean my soul and mind. I wash off all bad influences, bad thoughts and bad emotions. I clean myself completely by taking a shower on all three planes. I wash off all things which I do not want. And every time I use the toilet I leave all stress of my mind and soul. It feels natural to release all bad energies, all bad thoughts and emotions to the cool water when I wash myself and when I use the toilet. I automatically wipe off the uncleanliness of my mind and soul. It is a good habit to release the unwanted energies to the water flowing down the drain."

IMPREGNATION OF WATER

"I can easily impregnate cool water with my imagination, with my wishes, thoughts and feelings. It is like impregnating air, food and drinks. I just have to focus my imagination on the water and the water receives and keeps my wish. When I dip into the impregnated water the wish passes into my body, my mind and soul to realize. It feels natural and easy for me to impregnate cool water with my wishes and imagination."

AUTOSUGGESTION

"My subconsciousness supports me in my spiritual development, in reaching all my aims and ideals. My subconsciousness supports my refinement and the development of new abilities. My subconsciousness has a positive attitude and supports all my heart's desires. The work with my subconsciousness provides always good results and feels easy and natural for me. Intuitively I find the right words and formulation for my autosuggestions. My subconsciousness receives easily my wishes and works on their realization successfully."

SECOND STEP - SUGGESTIONS

SUMMARY OF EXERCISES OF STEP II:

Magic Mental Training:

1. Autosuggestion or the unveiled enigmas of the Unconscious.
2. Concentration Exercises:
    a) Visual (optical)
    b) Auditory
    c) Sensory
    d) Olfactory
    e) Taste

Exercises concerning the elimination of thoughts (negative state) are continued and deepened here.

Magic Psychic Training:

Magical-astral balance with respect to the elements, transmutation or refinement of character:

- a) by fight or control
- b) by autosuggestion
- c) by transmutation or transforming into the opposite quality.

Magic Physical Training:

1. Conscious pore breathing
2. Conscious position of the body (carriage)
3. Body control in everyday life, at will.

Before falling asleep, the most beautiful and purest ideas are to be taken along into the sleep.

MAGIC MENTAL TRAINING (II) – SUGGESTIONS

CONCENTRATION CAPACITY

"My capacity of concentration increases day by day naturally. With every concentration exercise my skills grow, refine and strengthen. With the natural development of my concentration capacity also my willpower improves daily, increases and strengthens. Day by day my concentration and will become better, stronger and finer."

Visual imagination

"My visual imagination skills unfold day by day more and more. It feels easy for me to use my visual imagination. My abilities in visual imagination increase, strengthen and refine daily with every exercise I do. My subconsciousness supports the development of my visual imagination skills so that they unfold in best way. I can memorize all details of an object easily and so it is easy to reproduce them in my imagination. The visual imagination is great and makes fun. I use it naturally each day and so I improve my skills permanently. It feels easy for me to visualize all kinds of objects."

Auditory imagination

"My auditory imagination skills unfold day by day more and more. It feels easy for me to use my auditory imagination. My abilities in auditory imagination increase, strengthen and refine daily with every exercise I do. My subconsciousness supports the development of my auditory imagination skills so that they unfold in best way. I can memorize all details of a sound or music easily and so it is easy to reproduce them in my imagination. The auditory imagination is great and makes fun. I use it naturally each day and so I improve my skills permanently. It feels easy for me to imagine all kinds of sounds."

Sensation imagination

"My sensation imagination skills unfold day by day more and more. It feels easy for me to use my sensation imagination. My abilities in sensation imagination increase, strengthen and refine daily with every exercise I do. My subconsciousness supports the development of my sensation imagination skills so that they unfold in best way. I can memorize all details of a sensation easily and so it is easy to reproduce them in my imagination. The sensation imagination is great and makes fun. I use it naturally each day and so I improve my skills permanently. It feels easy for me to imagine all kinds of sensations."

Olfactory imagination

"My olfactory imagination skills unfold day by day more and more. It feels easy for me to use my olfactory imagination. My abilities in olfactory imagination increase, strengthen and refine daily with every exercise I do. My subconsciousness supports the development of my olfactory imagination skills so that they unfold in best way. I can memorize all details of a fragrance easily and so it is easy to reproduce them in my imagination. The olfactory imagination is great and makes fun. I use it naturally each day and so I improve my skills permanently. It feels easy for me to imagine all kinds of fragrances."

Taste imagination

"My taste imagination skills unfold day by day more and more. It feels easy for me to use my taste imagination. My abilities in taste imagination increase, strengthen and refine daily with every exercise I do. My subconsciousness supports the development of my taste imagination skills so that they unfold in best way. I can memorize all details of a taste easily and so it is easy to reproduce them in my imagination. The taste imagination is great and makes fun. I use it naturally each day and so I improve my skills permanently. It feels easy for me to imagine all kinds of tastes."

Imagination with open eyes

"My imagination skills with all senses have been unfolding successfully day by day and so it feels easy for me to do my imagination exercises also with open eyes. My concentration works fine and I am able to imagine everything while my eyes are open. I am becoming a master in visual imagination, in auditory imagination, in sensation imagination and in taste imagination. Imagination with all senses has become a natural habit for me which I use every day successfully. Imagination is a great advantage in life."

Magic Psychic Training (II) – Suggestions

Systematical utilization of autosuggestion

"I use autosuggestion and autohypnosis systematically for all purposes in my spiritual training. My subconsciousness supports me in the realization of my magical abilities and mystical qualities. Using autosuggestion and autohypnosis makes my progress efficient and stable. My subconsciousness is well trained in the manifestation of my wishes. It is great to see how fast and successful my wishes realize thanks to the work of my subconsciousness."

Soul refinement

"Throughout the training I continue to work on the refinement of my character, of my personality. It feels good to refine myself, to unfold my higher nature. I know that there are several ways to cope with my bad characteristics, with my unwanted desires and bad habits. I know that I can use autosuggestion to reprogram my patterns of thinking, feeling and behavior. I know that it works well and that my subconsciousness supports me in my refinement process. Reprogramming myself is like setting good seeds where the weeds have been and to make them grow. Alternatively I can directly fight and control bad behavior by using my strong will. I know that my willpower is stronger than any kind of bad habit, bad characteristic or bad behavior. With my strong will I am able to block the bad before it starts to break out or to show up. And so it loses its power and vanishes by itself. Even if there is a strong energy which tries to break out I know that I just have to wait some moments until the energy decreases naturally so that I can keep the control. But I have also a third option. By deep meditation I can transmute the bad quality into the opposite quality. Indeed this is also a form of self-hypnosis. I meditate about the bad behavior or habit and analyze in which situation it occurs, how it feels, which key stimulus is necessary to provoke my behavior. Then I imagine the same situation, the same key stimulus but with a positive behavior. So I change reality. I make a new, positive experience which lets me react in a positive way the next time the situation occurs. The better my imagination and meditation works the better and easier the change will be later in reality. And the energy which I used for the unwanted behavior transmutes into the energy for the positive behavior. My subconsciousness and my meditation help me to perform this transformation. It is alchemy and it is just a matter of my imagination, my willpower and intention. For my progress and refinement I use all techniques successfully. I follow my intuition which technique fits best for the single problem. It is great to experience how I refine myself day by day and how all my problems vanish more and more."

MAGIC PHYSICAL TRAINING (II) – SUGGESTIONS

CONSCIOUS PORE-BREATHING

"I have learned to observe my deep natural breathing, how my chest and belly move when I inhale and exhale in a natural rhythm. While I keep this natural breathing I can focus my imagination on the idea that also my whole body inhales and exhales, that from all sides vital energy enters my body when I inhale and that wasted energies pour out when I exhale. I inhale vital energies from all sides with my whole body and I exhale wasted energies to all sides with my whole body. It feels more and more easy and natural for me to inhale and to exhale with my whole body. I can feel the vital energy entering my skin and I can feel when the energy leaves my body. I know that not my physical body is breathing. It is my energetic body which is able to inhale and to exhale vital energy, indeed all kinds of energy. It is all a matter of my imagination and will. The energies always follow my intention. Day by day I become more and more a master of vital energy and pore-breathing. It feels so natural to breath with the whole body. I know that I can impregnate the vital energy which surrounds me with my wishes like I do it with air, food and drinks. Pore-breathing allows me to draw in big amounts of energy which are enriched with my wishes, my will and imagination. I can easily combine the breathing with my lungs with pore-breathing and my natural breathing. If I like I can also focus only on the exhaling of bad characteristics, stress, wasted energies, etc. with my whole body. My intuition shows me the diversity of possibilities and techniques which I can use for breathing and the work with vital energy."

CONTROL OF YOUR BODY

"I can sit still and comfortable in my asana. My spine remains straight. My feet are kept together so that they form a right angle with my knees. My body feels relaxed and my hands rest on my thighs. It feels really comfortable for me. While my physical body can relax completely I can concentrate on my psychic work, on my meditations and mental exercises. My body gets used to the asana more and more each day so that my body automatically relaxes when I take my asana. So I do not really need time to calm down. In contrary I get easily and automatically in the right state of mind for meditation as soon as my body is in the asana. The body posture works really great for me and supports all my spiritual work and training."

CONTROL OVER NEEDS

"I have full control over all needs of my body. Regarding the principle mind-over-matter I am the master of my body and I am in control of all needs and desires. Certainly I take good care of my body to keep it healthy and fit."

BEFORE SLEEP

"Before falling asleep, I cultivate the most beautiful and purest ideas in my mind and take them into my sleep. These wonderful and pure ideas serve my inner harmony and my refinement and I sleep very well every night."

THIRD STEP - SUGGESTIONS

SUMMARY OF EXERCISES OF STEP III

Magic Mental Training

1. Concentration on thoughts with two or three senses at once.
2. Concentration on objects, landscapes, places.
3. Concentration on animals and human beings.

Magic Psychic Training

Inhaling of the elements in the whole body:

a) Fire - warmth
b) Air - lightness
c) Water - coolness
d) Earth - heaviness

Magic Physical Training

1. Retaining of Step I, which has to become a habit
2. Accumulation of vital power:

- a. by breathing through the lungs and pores in the whole body
- b. in the different parts of the body

Appendix to Step III:

1. Impregnation of space for reasons of health, success, &c.
2. Biomagnetism

Magic mental training (III) – suggestions

The four pillars of Solomon's temple

"I know how important the four pillars of Solomon's temple are. Knowledge, daring, volition and silence are the pillars of real mastership, of the divine temple which realizes in my personality. All four pillars I develop and integrate them continuously day by day in my personality. Knowledge, daring, volition and silence grow and unfold completely in my microcosm so that I reach mastership and make good progress every day."

Concentration with 2-3 senses at once

"I have become used to the imagination with all my senses. It feels easy and natural for me to use my imagination with the single senses. I feel that I am able to use 2-3 senses at once for my imagination. This enhances my training and I love to do it. It is easy for me to concentrate on one thing while I use several senses at the same time. My imagination becomes vivid. Day by day I become more and more used to the concentration with several senses at once. My imagination works better and better and I am really happy for the good results. I can imagine all kinds of objects, locations, moving animals and humans. It brings so much fun and feels so real. My imagination develops perfectly so that I am also able to imagine the objects with open eyes. It is amazing and I am so thankful for these great skills."

Magic psychic training (III) – suggestions

Breathing of the elements

"Like I am able to breathe vital energy with my lungs and my whole body, I am able to breathe the four elements with their different sensational qualities. The fire element is warm, expansive energy, the air element is airy, light energy, the water element is cool energy and the earth element is heavy, dense energy. Due to my imagination exercises regarding the diversity of sensations it feels easy for me to focus on the sensations of the four elements. Easily I can imagine myself in the center of an element energy with the according sensation. And with my concentration skills I can strengthen the sensation so that it manifests also on the astral plane, that I can really feel it. As I am used to pore-breathing it feels natural and easy for me to inhale and to exhale the element energies. After each exercise I can dissolve the element energy completely from my body into the universe where I dissolve it too. The element energies wash my mind, my soul, my energetic body. They clean me, they heal me, they harmonize me, they refine me and they help me to gain complete mastership in the controlling of and work with the four elements. Indeed the breathing exercises with the four elements is true alchemistic work which helps me to refine myself to high degrees. I become more and more used to the energies of the elements in my microcosm day by day. It feels natural and easy to work with the elements in my soul and body."

Magic physical training (III) – suggestions

Breathing of vital energy with body parts

"Due to my intensive training of breathing vital energy with my lungs and also my whole body I am used to charge myself and any kinds of objects with vital energy. It is just a matter of my will and imagination. In fact I can charge everything with vital energy independent from time and space, independent from size, form and visibility. It is all a matter of my imagination. The energy follows always my intention. So far I have charged my whole body with vital energy but it is also easy to charge the regions and the parts of my body. I just have to focus my attention on the region or part of my body which I want to charge and then I imagine how it inhales and exhales the vital energy which is in the environment. So I am able to let my fingers breathe, my hands, feet, my legs, my head, my arms, my torso, my chest, my belly, etc. It feels completely easy and natural for me to breathe with all parts and regions of my body – inhaling and exhaling of vital energy, so simple. I can really feel how the vital energy enters from all sides for example my hand and how it is exhaled back into the environment. It makes fun to train this ability. The more I do this training the easier it becomes to charge any kind of body part or region. I experience also the vitalizing effect of this exercise. It is very healthy."

Breathing of Vital Energy with Organs

"In the same way I have trained the breathing of vital energy with body parts and regions I can do it with all of my organs. I just have to focus on the form and appearance of an organ so that I connect my mind to it and then I let it breathe in my imagination, let it inhale and exhale. For example I focus on the appearance of my right kidney and imagine now how it inhales vital energy and how it exhales vital energy. While I do so I can feel how the vital energy enters my kidney and how it is exhaled from it. In fact it is as easy as all other breathing exercises. I know that I use here the Akasha principle automatically which bridges space to let my hidden organs inhale and exhale the vital energy of the universe directly. It makes fun to work with all organs, to remember their appearance and form, and also the location of them. Indeed it is really easy to let all organs breathe vital energy."

Accumulation of Vital Energy

"Meanwhile I am a master in letting all organs, body parts, body regions and any kind of objects and other beings breathe vital energy. I can make everything inhale and exhale energy. I know that there are different kinds of energy like fresh vital energy and the opposite wasted or ill energy. So it is also easy for me to let parts of my body inhale good, fresh energies and exhale bad, wasted energies. It is just a matter of my imagination, my mental focus. And so I can increase the health of body parts, organs, etc. by inhaling fresh energy and exhaling bad energy. But this is not all. I can also accumulate vital energy in all parts, objects and beings. This is quite simple. I just have to keep the inhalation of energy while I exhale vacantly. So I increase the amount of energy in my body, body part and region or in any other object. After a while I focus then on the decreasing of the gathered energy so that the charged object returns to the normal level of energy. The process of charging is quite easy. Due to my training my whole body and all parts and organs become used to high amounts of energy.

This strengthens my energetic structure, my nerves and it increases my natural level of vital energy and certainly my charisma and my health. Also my wishes realize much faster now. This all feels great and I am thankful for my progress."

Emission of energy at once

"I am trained in decreasing the accumulation of energy step by step with each time I exhale. But I know that I can also emit the whole energy at once. It is explosive like a bursting balloon or tire. I just have to focus my concentration on this explosive emission of energy and then does it happen. It is like opening a valve and the energy will emit due to the high pressure. Doing my training in this form makes it natural and easy for me to emit all energy at once especially from my hands and fingers. I know that it is all only a matter of training and repetition. A matter of will and imagination. Training leads always to mastership."

Special application of accumulation

"I can use the accumulation of vital energy for special purposes. I can charge my hands to use them for the imposition of hands to let the energy flow into my patient, into ill body parts. I can also use my charged hands to bless my food, my drinks or to bless other people. When I charge my eyes with vital energy, they become fascinating for other people. This increases my influence on them. And certainly I can increase my charisma when I charge myself completely. The accumulation of energy in myself, in others and in objects provides a diversity of good applications. My intuition leads me automatically to the right forms of application."

Space impregnation

"I am able to charge any kinds of rooms or objects and to impregnate them with my will, thoughts and feelings. It doesn´t matter at all if I charge an organ, my whole body, an object or a whole room. It is always the same procedure, only a matter of will and imagination. So I just have to focus my attention on a room, a space or object and then I can let it breathe or charge with vital energy. I know that I can impregnate the charged space with my wishes, my thoughts and my feelings. I can assign all kinds of ideas, energetic states and emotions to the vital energy. I can program the vital energy with determinations of time and dimensions, with orders and conditions. Space impregnation is a fascinating topic. My intuition shows me the different useful applications of charging spaces. I know that I can support my health, my well-being, success, good sleep, healing, good concentration and a lot of other things with space impregnation. It is indeed a great tool."

FORTH STEP - SUGGESTIONS

Summary of exercises of step IV

Magic Mental Training:

1. Transplantation of consciousness:
    a. into objects
    b. into animals
    c. into human beings

Magic Psychic Training:

1. Accumulation of elements:
    a. in the whole body
    b. in single parts of the body with the help of two methods

2. Production of element harmony in the appropriate regions of the body:
    a. Fire - head
    b. Air - chest
    c. Water - abdomen, belly
    d. Earth - pelvis, genitals, legs and feet

Magic Physical Training:

1. Rituals & their practical applicability:
    a. gesticulations (gestures)
    b. bearings
    c. postures of the fingers (mudras)

MAGIC MENTAL TRAINING (IV) – SUGGESTIONS

TRANSFERRING OF CONSCIOUSNESS

"I know that my mind, my consciousness is independent from time and space. There are no limits for my mind. My consciousness can travel the whole universe without any problems. It can travel into the past and into the future. It can take every form or shape. It can connect and move into every object or being. There are not limitations for my consciousness. My consciousness is just used to stay in my body and so I must train its natural abilities. The training of the transfer and connection of my mind with every kind of object, animal and human being is as usual just a matter of my imagination. So I focus on the object; I imagine that I become one with it and that I take its form and place. Doing this I withdraw my perception of being me. This is a little bit strange but the more I train this, the easier it becomes and the more natural it feels for me. Indeed it becomes a habit and it is very interesting to perceive the world from a different perspective. With each repetition I get easier into touch with the mental and astral sphere of the object, animal or human being I train with and so I can take part in its mental activity, its thoughts, qualities, feelings and its energetic state. This serves my intuition, my perception of others, my understanding of others. I can also connect easier to other beings and objects in everyday life. And I can influence them easier with my thoughts and positive suggestions. When I step in the imagination of an object, animal or human being I become one with it for the time of training. I take part in its nature. But then I can leave it and return completely back to being me, to my real personality. The more I train this the easier it is. It is all a matter of imagination. It is like making a step forward – suddenly you are in a new place. I become more and more aware of the abilities and the true nature of my consciousness. My mind is unlimited, free from time and space. I can move wherever I want to be and I can take every form and shape I want. And indeed I can become whatever I wish for. So I can examine all forms of life, all kinds of beings. I can enhance my understanding of creation and creatures. The transfer of my consciousness becomes easier day by day and I am happy to be blessed with such a great ability."

Magic psychic training (IV) – suggestions

Element accumulation

"Like I am used to breathe vital energy into my body, body parts and organs, I can breathe and accumulate the energies of the four elements. My imagination is just focused on the quality of the specific element and besides this it is the same process. So what I am able to perform with the vital energy, I am able to do with the four elements. I can imagine myself in the center of the fire element where the energy is warm and expansive. I can inhale this fiery energy with my lungs and my whole body. I can accumulate the energy by drawing the energy without exhaling it. I can let my body parts and organs breathe the element energies. And certainly I can accumulate the element energies in all body parts and organs. The more I do my training the easier and natural it feels for me to work with the four elements in the same way that I do with the vital energy. It becomes more and more a good habit. From day to day my mastership in working with vital energy and the four elements increases. I especially focus the accumulation of the elements in my hands, fingers and feet as I know that I need this ability as a magician. The more exercises I do the easier it feels to return the charged element energies at once back to the universe. It is exactly the same like I am trained with vital energy. It is like opening a valve and suddenly the energies emit to the universe."

ELEMENT BREATHING WITH CONSCIOUSNESS TRANSFER

"I know that I can use the Akasha principle to let body parts and organs breathe or to accumulate energy in them. I just have to transfer my mind into the body part or organ and so I am able to inhale energies from all sides being in the center point respectively being the organ itself. I have trained the transfer of my consciousness very well and I am trained in taking the shape or appearance of an object. So it feels easy and natural to transfer my consciousness in whatever I want and let it inhale and exhale the energies of the elements. It is all a matter of imagination. I can ease the exercise by imagining myself as the organ in the center of vital energy or one of the four elements without the rest of my body. Then I can easily inhale, exhale and accumulate the energies. Day by day I improve my abilities to real mastership in all my magical abilities. And so I become naturally and automatically a master of breathing vital energy and the energies of the four elements."

MAGICAL EQUILIBRIUM

"Due to my training with the four elements I am protected against the pernicious influence of the negative side of the elements. Having achieved the magical equipoise I am standing in the center of all events and I will be aware of all the laws, all the constitutive moments and processes taking place in the universe, in the true perspective. I am spared from many illnesses producing an effect of balance on my own karma and thus on my fate; I become more and more resistant against any dangerous influences. I am cleaning my mental and astral aura, strengthening my mental and astral matrix. I am reviving my magical faculties and my intuition has an universal character. My astral senses are more and more refined and my intellectual capacities rise. Mastering the four elements in my whole microcosm blesses me with a great inner harmony and peace. I feel centered in myself and in my life. I feel saturated with the powers and qualities of the four elements and this makes me feel free and independent. I am thankful for the experience of the magical equilibrium and true mastership over the four elements."

MAGICAL PHYSICAL TRAINING (IV) – SUGGESTIONS

ASCETICISM

"I can stick firmly to any asceticism I impose upon myself without having to fight temptations or even to succumb to any of them. My will is strong and I am saturated by the elements and vital energy. So I am free to follow any kind of asceticism as I think it is right and useful."

Asana

"I can keep my body posture, my asana for hours without feeling the slightest disturbance, nervousness, tension or convulsion. My body has become used to my asana. My body can relax completely in this body posture while I am busy on the mental and astral plane."

The power of radiation

"I enforce and deepen my power of radiation day by day naturally. My radiation becomes more expansive and more dynamic each day automatically. Intuitively I learn the practical use of the radiant power for any purpose and in any situation. I reach such a degree of perfection that any desire that I set into my radiant power is realized instantly. My power of radiation becomes stronger each day, improves and refines with every exercise I do. My charisma is astonishing and lets me realize all my wishes quickly. My level of energy is at least ten times higher than the one of normal people. I am indeed a power station."

Rituals

"I intuitively find the fitting gestures and finger postures to express ideas for the magical application. I know that I can express by rituals all kinds of ideas or trains of thoughts. By using the ritual consciously I connect the idea and magical operation to the gesture or finger posture. Training this connection makes it work automatically so that after a while it is enough to use the ritual to cause the connected effects. It makes fun to combine and train the ritual with the magical operation so that it becomes a habit. I know that effective rituals are just a matter of repetition, of consciously training at the beginning and the automated use later. I can create for all purposes the right rituals. My intuition leads me always to the fitting ideas."

ELEMENTS AND FINGERS

"In analogy to the five elements I assign the fire element to the forefinger, the water element to the thumb, the Akasha element to the middle finger, the earth element to the ring finger and the air element to the little finger. The right hand represents the positive elements and the left one the negative elements. Intuitively I find the fitting rituals and gestures to operate with all elements, to accumulate them and to dissolve them. My intuition leads me to the right solutions."

FIFTH STEP - SUGGESTIONS

SUMMARY OF EXERCISES OF STEP V

Magic Mental Training

1. Space Magic

Magic Psychic Training

1. Projection of elements outwards:
    a. through the body, accumulated through the solar plexus
    b. accumulated through the hands, especially dynamically through the fingers.

Magic Physical Training

1. Preparation for the passive communication with the invisible ones:
   a. release of the hand
   b. preparation of the fingers with the help of the pendulum, pencil, planchette, etc.
2. Passive Communication:
   a. with the own spiritual guide
   b. with deceased people and other beings.

Magic Mental Training (V) – Suggestions

Transfer of Consciousness into the Akasha Point

"I am trained in transferring my consciousness into every kind of object, body part or organ. So it feels easy and natural for me to transfer my consciousness also into the depth-point, the center of my body. It is the Akasha point, the point which provides total control over my microcosm. It is indeed the control and center point of every being and every object. I can set my mind into the depth-point of myself, of all beings and objects. When I do so I can imagine myself, my consciousness as small as a seed, as small as an atom, so that the object is as big as a whole universe. As usual it is all a matter of my imagination. I can do it with symmetrical objects as well as with unsymmetrical ones. With these exercises I gain more and more the ability to comprehend all kinds of objects and beings from their center. I comprehend their core, their nature. Further on I have the ability to influence every object from the nucleus, to load it magically at will, and thus to impregnate the mental sphere of every object with my desire. I can do this also with animals, human beings and with objects which are not directly in front of my eyes. The work with the Akasha point feels more and more easy and natural for me."

The determining power

"When I transfer my consciousness into the middle of my body, into the pit of my stomach, the solar plexus I feel and know that I am the center of my body, that I am the determining power in my microcosm. I am the master and the determining power of my whole microcosm on all three planes. I am able to transfer my consciousness at any hour and in every situation into my depth-point, into my Akasha principle. There I can perceive and influence all that concerns my nature. I know that this consciousness transference into the Akasha principle is the genuine magical state of trance which I can enter at will any time I want to."

Magic psychic training (V) – suggestions

Projection of the elements through the solar plexus

"I am trained now in the accumulation of vital energy and the four elements. I am also trained in emitting them at once back into the universe. So I am well prepared to let them flow through my solar plexus as well. I can discharge myself easily through my solar plexus or my hands, fingers and feet. When I have accumulated a kind of energy then I can let it flow through my solar plexus into a room to fill it completely. When I do so I become empty and the energy is spread into the room. This is quite easy and as always just a matter of my developed imagination. With the same ease I can accumulate any kind of energy in my hands or fingers and then let if fill a whole room or an object. So I can discharge myself immediately and charge something directly to program it with my wish. I can also create all kinds of imagined objects in my solar plexus with the accumulated energy. I can create balls, cubes, pyramids, cones, also complex forms, indeed everything I want. It is just a matter of my well-trained imagination. I can charge these imagined objects with energy. I can also accumulate the energy in these forms. Then I can send them or project them outwards wherever I like."

Projection of the elements directly from the universe

"I can project the elements directly from the universe. I just have to draw the element energy from the endless space, the universe, and fill with it a room or object. I know that the energy or element is quite fine coming from the primary source. It is quite etheric and subtle but the more I draw it into an object or room the denser and stronger it becomes. The element qualities can be really felt then. The more I train the process of accumulating and condensing energies the easier it becomes for me to materialize them. Day by day my abilities to condense and accumulate energies increase more and more."

Magical physical training (V) – suggestions

Comment in advance

With this comment I want to question the exercise of Bardon a little bit to ease your training. You have at least two options for the training of your hand for automatic writing. In the first one you really work on the levitation of your hand and arm like Bardon suggests. In the second one you train your subconsciousness to receive the necessary impulses for writing by your spiritual guide. This first aim can take you months or years as Bardon states by himself that the physical mastership over the elements takes years of training. Indeed you are meant to accumulate the air element to physical degrees to be able to levitate hand and arm. When you compare this hard work and long effort with the small result of automatic writing then it makes no sense – especially as you will unfold your higher senses soon to be able to communicate with your spiritual guide directly.

So with my hypnotherapeutic background I interpret Bardon´s explanations in the second way – as the work with the subconsciousness of hand and arm. Here the exercise is much easier and the effort is okay regarding the benefit. I explain this: You can imagine that your fingers, hand and arm move and levitate without a normal direct impulse of your will. Your subconsciousness follows your imagination and moves them. You have indeed the impression that an external power is responsible for these movements. When you are in a meditative trance state like being in hypnosis you can train this easily and you will have success. Hypnotherapists often use the levitation of arms as a tool for their sessions. As soon as your subconsciousness is trained to move fingers, hand and arms according to your imagination then your spiritual guide can do the same. He can use his imagination and his mental hand to control your hand for writing and communicating. For success most important are the preparation/training of your subconsciousness to follow your imagination and certainly a good state of trance, meditation. Then you can move your mental hand and arm out of your physical one and you are ready to call your spiritual guide to enter with his hand for communication.

By the way – automatic writing is not unusual for the direct communication with the subconsciousness of a person in hypnotherapy and coaching. It is just a small step to use this for the communication with spiritual guides and deceased persons.

Certainly it is up to you how you follow Bardon´s explanations.

LEVITATION EXERCISES

"Using my will and imagination in the state of meditative trance I can lift and drop all my fingers of my right hand. I can also lift and drop all my fingers of my left hand. My subconsciousness follows my will and imagination and moves my fingers. Due to my training I am also able to lift and drop my hands and my arms. My subconsciousness is well prepared to follow my will and imagination. I know that my subconsciousness controls all functions of my body and so it is able to levitate my fingers, hands and arms when I imagine this. Now my subconsciousness is well prepared and moves my fingers, hands and arms according to the impulses of will and imagination. So they are ready to receive the will and imagination of my spiritual guide for moving my hands for automatic writing. My spiritual guide can control my fingers, hands and arms with his will and his mental hand. And so we can communicate in a successful way."

EXTERIORIZING OF THE MENTAL HAND

"I know that I can concentrate myself on my mental hand with the mental fingers and the mental arm. When I lead my sensation to my mental hand I can use my imagination to loosen it from the physical hand and to exteriorize it. I can put my mental hand onto my thigh so that my physical hand becomes empty. Now my physical hand is ready to be filled and used by the mental hand of my spiritual guide. He can enter my physical hand like a glove and then he is able to use it to write with it or to give signs with my fingers. I know that the communication with my spiritual guide is important to learn all I want to know and to receive everything I am in need of. Due to my good preparation my spiritual guide can use my hands easily for a successful communication via finger signs, pendulum and automatic writing. I know that I can also invite deceased friends, relatives and members of my family with whom I want to get in touch. They all can see my exteriorized hand and certainly they all can use my physical hand and fingers to communicate with me. From exercise to exercise I become more and more a master of the communication with the higher realms and the mediumistic writing feels easier and easier each day."

SIXTH STEP - SUGGESTIONS

SUMMARY OF EXERCISES OF STEP VI

Magic Mental Training:

1. Meditation on the own spirit
2. Becoming conscious of the senses in the spirit

Magic Psychic Training:

1. Preparation to master the Akasha principle
2. Deliberate induction to trance with the help of the Akasha
3. Mastering of the elements with the help of an individual ritual from the Akasha

Magic Physical Training:

1. Deliberate creation of beings
    a. Elementals
    b. Larvae
    c. Phantasms (shadows)
    d. Phantoms

Magic mental training (VI) – suggestions

The four elements in the mind

"When I meditate about the four principles of my mind according to the elements I comprehend deeply that my will and motivation belongs to the fire element, that the intellect with intelligence and memory underlies the principle of air, that sensation and feeling belongs to the water element and the consciousness which connects the three elements is subordinated to the earth principle. The more I meditate about the functions of my consciousness the deeper I understand all aspects and processes of my mind. The deeper I understand them the better I can influence these functions with the respective element on the mental plane in myself as well as in others, to master and to strengthen or to eliminate them. Here it is all a matter of a deep understanding and differentiation between the four elements and their work in the mind. The influence is just a matter of my will, my imagination and the work with the elements."

Differentiation between the three bodies

"By deep meditation and training I am able to differentiate between my mental body, my astral body and my physical body. I know that my original being is the mental body, the spirit, which is very fine. It is my feeling, my sensation, my awareness. I, my mental being, am in a fine astral body and with my astral body I am in my material body, the densest appearance of myself. It is comparable with a hand in a fine silk glove which is put into a thick glove. Both gloves can be felt by the hand as they differ in density. The more I train the better I can focus my attention on the different bodies and planes. I can really feel that I am originally a mental being in an astral and physical body."

Conscious Actions

"Thanks to my developed differentiation between the three planes of my existence, my mental, astral and physical body I am able to accomplish actions fully consciously. I imagine and feel that my spirit is accomplishing all actions with the help of my soul and my material body. This awareness lets me do things in a totally conscious way, in a magical way so that I can perform work on the mental, astral and physical plane at the same time. It is also useful to work consciously with my mental and astral senses on the higher planes. When I walk I know that my mental being walks in the astral body moving the material body. When I see then I know that my mental eyes see with the help of my astral eyes looking with my material eyes. The astral sensory organs pass on the perception of the material senses to my spirit, my mental senses. The more I train this differentiation the more I become aware of these facts and the easier I can concentrate myself on this process. I can concentrate myself on all five senses in the same way. I can differentiate the work of my mental, astral and physical eyes, my mental, astral and physical ears, my feeling and my olfactory sense and taste. I can develop the differentiation for all my senses. Day by day I become more and more aware of the differences between my mental sense, my astral senses and my physical senses and how they all work together. I gain full mastership in the concentration on my mental body and senses, my astral body and senses and my physical body with his senses. I know that I, the mental being, control my astral body and my physical body. I can easily switch between these three planes, bodies and senses."

Magic Psychic Training (VI) – Suggestions

Total Mastership over the Four Elements

"I have got the faculty of mastering the elements due to my intensive training. I know that they will fulfill everything I order or wish for, no matter on which plane the realization of my desires has to happen. I feel the total mastery of the elements. I have absolute faith and confidence in my total control of the elements. I am capable of projecting the elements on all planes very easily, outwards as well as inwards so that all seems to be a child's play to me. I know that I can transfer the power of the elements into a suitable ritual. My divine intuition will guide me to choose the fitting ritual for it. I know that I can use finger positions, gestures, self-selected words, formulas and sounds corresponding to the elements regarding the Quabbalah. I know that the rituals are absolutely individual and purely personal. So I am absolutely successful in the making of a fitting ritual for the total power of the elements."

Comment

It makes sense to use autohypnosis for each single ritual which you have created. As Bardon states the student should create one ritual for the accumulation and one for the dissolving of an element on the astral and on the material plane. In sum these are 16 rituals. I recommend to make also rituals for the mental plane regarding the mental qualities of the elements. Then you have 24 rituals. Besides this it is useful to make two rituals for the control of the vital energy and later for light and the fluids. As a last hint – it makes sense to create the rituals as easy and good to perform as possible so that you can use them perfectly.

Magic Physical Training (VI) – Suggestions

Creation of Elementals

"My intuition and inspiration work perfectly to create elementals for any purpose. I intuitively know how to prepare myself, how to plan the process, how to choose the right program, etc. My divine guidance is perfect and I am happy that I do everything in the right and successful way. My elementals work as they are supposed to do and I am 100 % satisfied with their performance."

Seventh Step - Suggestions

Summary of exercises of step VII

Magic Mental Training:

1. Analysis of the spirit with respect to the practice.

Magic Psychic Training:

1. Development of the astral senses with the help of elements and fluid condensers.
    a. clairvoyance
    b. clairaudience
    c. clairfeeling

Magic Physical Training:

1. Creation of elementaries with the help of four different methods
2. Magic animation of pictures.

MAGIC MENTAL TRAINING (VII) – SUGGESTIONS

ANALYSIS OF THE SPIRIT

"It feels easy for me to analyze my spirit and to find out which of the elements is predominant in my mind. I know that I have to cause a perfect balance of the elements by suitable concentration exercises and deep meditation. Day by day the balance of the elements in mental body and consciousness improves automatically. So a perfect harmony with regard to the elements develops more and more in my spirit."

MAGIC PSYCHIC TRAINING (VII) – SUGGESTIONS

DEVELOPMENT OF THE ASTRAL SENSES

"All my astral senses develop naturally so that I am able to see, hear, feel, smell and taste on the astral plane. My astral senses unfold due to my intensive work with the elements and my concentration exercises. I support their refinement and development by my special training for each single sense. My clairvoyance improves and refines by the accumulation of light in my eyeballs. The light contains all qualities and abilities of clairvoyance and my eyes become used to it. So my clairvoyance unfolds naturally and perfectly. I am able to see everything I want to over time and space.

My clairaudience develops and improves by the accumulation of the air element in my ears. So I am able to hear voices even at the remotest distance and, at the same time, to understand the language of all beings. With the accumulation of the water element I improve and refine my clairsentience. So I am able to feel on the astral plane all kinds of energies and qualities. Day by day my astral senses unfold more and more and I become used to activate my astral senses to see, feel and hear on the astral plane bridging time and space. My perception is unlimited thanks to my astral senses. I am happy about the perfect and complete unfolding and refinement of all my astral senses."

MAGIC PHYSICAL TRAINING (VII) – SUGGESTIONS

CREATION OF ELEMENTARIES

"My intuition and inspiration work perfectly to create elementaries for any purpose. I intuitively know how to prepare myself, how to plan the process, how to choose the right program, etc. My divine guidance is perfect and I am happy that I do everything in the right and successful way. My elementaries work as they are supposed to do and I am 100 % satisfied with their performance."

ANIMATION OF PICTURES

"I am able to animate pictures as I like to. My intuition and inspiration work perfectly to animate pictures for any purposes. I intuitively know how to prepare them well for full success."

EIGHTH STEP - SUGGESTIONS

Summary of exercises of step VIII

Magic Mental Training:

1. Preparation for mental wandering
2. Practice of mental wandering
    a. in the room
    b. short distances
    c. visits to friends, relatives, etc.

Magic Psychic Training:

1. The great NOW
2. No clinging to the past
3. Concentration disturbances as a compass of the magic equilibrium
4. The astral body and the light
5. Mastering of the electric and magnetic fluids

Magic Physical Training:

1. Magic influence through the elements
2. Fluid condensers:
    a. simple condensers
    b. compound condensers
    c. fluid condensers for magic mirrors
    d. preparation of a magic mirror with the help of fluid condensers

Magic mental training (VIII) – suggestions

Mental wandering

"I am able to leave my body with my mental being in the same way as a pigeon leaves the dovecote. I can easily leave my physical body to betake myself anywhere else, where I will see, hear and feel everything. There is no material hindrance for me, neither time nor space exists for my spirit and I can rush around the whole world in a single moment if I like to. For mental wandering I imagine myself like an image in a mirror and then I place my mind, my mental being into this mental form, image of myself. Then I am able to move in this body like I am used to in my physical body. Certainly I am not limited to physical actions but indeed I can use the laws of the mental plane to move without any limitations of time and space. I am able to step out of my body according to my will. I have a deep sensation of inner liberty and self-determination. I can walk in my flat. I can sit. I can do my gymnastics in my mental body. I can visit all rooms in my flat. I also can walk outside. Due to my intensive training I am able to use consciously the laws of the mental realms. So I can fly and float in the air. I can move through walls and ceilings. I can change my size and my appearance by imagination. I can travel by intention. I just have to think about a place and I am there. I can go into the ocean, into the earth and into the air to discover their mental realms. For my mental being there are no limits, no limits of time or space. The elevation to other spheres is also very simple. I only have to concentrate on the sphere that I like to visit. Then I be lifted up vertically like through a funnel. I know that I just have to focus on a place or sphere to be there immediately. In this way I can also meet other beings. I concentrate on the being and I am immediately in front of it. The more I train mental traveling the easier and more natural it feels for me. Day by day I become more and more used to mental traveling."

MAGIC PSYCHIC TRAINING (VIII) – SUGGESTIONS

THE NOBLE MAGICIAN

"Being a magician I always foster pure and noble thoughts and endeavor to transmute passions into good qualities. I am so refined in my personality that I am no longer capable of evil thoughts or of wishing anything bad to other people. I am always kind, obliging and willing to help at any time, to assist by word and deed, to act generously, considerately and discretely. I am free from ambition, superciliousness and I avoid any boasting. Thanks to my hard training and the refinement of my soul I adapt myself more and more to the Akasha principle which provides a deep harmony in all aspects of life. As a genuine magician I take life as it is; I enjoy the good things and learn from the bad ones, but I will never give up. I am aware of my own weaknesses and I try to overcome them. But I ignore any thoughts of repentance, since they are negative thoughts that are to be avoided. It is sufficient to recognize my own faults and never to relapse into them again. So I live, if possible, exclusively in the present, looking back only if the need arises. I will limit any plans concerning his future to the most urgent and keep away from fantasy and daydreaming. Nor will I waste my abilities acquired in hard work or give the subconscious any chance to handicap me. As a magician I work purposefully on my development without neglecting my material duties, which I fulfill just as scrupulously as the task of my spiritual progress. Since the Akasha principle ignores time and space, acting permanently in the present time, for the concept of time depends on our senses, I adapt myself as much as possible to Akasha. I acknowledge the great moment of NOW as representative. I think and act according to it."

Magical balance

"Day by day I realize the magical balance more and more in my microcosm. More and more I am able to manage equally all kinds of concentration with my senses. I can keep any imagination in my mind for at least 15 minutes without the slightest disturbance, no matter which of the elements is concerned."

Mastering of the light

"Like vital energy and the elements, light is another form of energy which I can handle easily in the same way. I can charge myself and other objects with light. I can inhale and exhale it. I can accumulate light. I can charge organs, body parts and whole rooms with light. I can program it for all my purposes. It is easy for me to work with light. Day by day I increase my mastership in the control of light."

Mastering of the fluids

"Like all energies before I can control the electric and magnetic fluids better and better with each day of training. I can charge myself and other objects with the fluids. I can inhale and exhale them. I can accumulate them. I can charge organs, body parts and whole rooms with the electric and magnetic fluids. I can program them for all my purposes. It is easy for me to work with the fluids. Day by day I increase my mastership in the use of the electric and magnetic fluids. As a master of the two universal powers I can achieve practically everything."

Increasing of Abilities (Electric Fluid)

"The electric fluid reinforces and increases all my active powers in spirit, soul and body. The electric fluid arouses, increases and strengthens all active faculties, qualities, etc., that are imputed to the fire element and the air element in myself. The electric fluid increases my will power, my faith and my control of the elements to a supernatural degree."

Increasing of Abilities (Magnetic Fluid)

"The magnetic fluid reinforces and increases all my passive powers in spirit, soul and body. The magnetic fluid arouses, increases and strengthens all passive faculties, qualities, etc., that are imputed to the water element and the earth element in myself. The magnetic fluid increases my mediumistic faculties, clairfeeling, psychometry, thought reading, medial writing and others to a supernatural degree."

Fluids for Healing

"Charging my right hand with the electrical fluid and my left hand with the magnetic fluid I am able to heal myself and others in a most powerful way. My divine intuition guides me in all healing treatments with the two fluids. I am aware of the great chances to heal people by the use of these universal powers."

Magic physical training (VIII) – suggestions

Comment in advance

For the purposes of step VIII there are no real suggestions which could be created. Bardon describes techniques but no abilities. On the other hand you can prepare your subconsciousness for the successful and intuitive work with the presented techniques. It is up to you if you think you benefit.

Direct use of the elements

"I know how to use the elements directly for self-influencing as well as for influencing other people. I can realize my wishes with the fire element by combustion, with the air element by evaporation, the water element by mixture and with the earth element by decomposition. In all my magical operations I am guided and inspired by my divine intuition. So I gain always full success in all tasks and operations."

Fluid condensers

"I am able to make fluid condensers. My intuition guides me. The work is interesting and makes fun. I become easily familiar with making good fluid condensers. I know how to apply them for my purposes and it is great to experience how good they work."

Magic mirrors

"I am able to prepare and to use magic mirrors successfully. My intuition guides me. I know how to charge them, to prepare them in the right way to fulfill their purpose. The work with the magic mirrors is fascinating and they are really useful for many operations."

NINTH STEP - SUGGESTIONS

SUMMARY OF EXERCISES OF STEP IX

Magic Mental Training:

1. Practice of clairvoyance with the help of magic mirrors
   a. seeing through time and space
   b. distant effect through the magic mirror
   c. different tasks of projection through the magic mirror

Magic Psychic Training:

1. Deliberate separation of the astral body from the material body
2. Impregnation of the astral body with the four divine fundamental qualities.

Magic Physical Training:

1. Treatment of the sick with the electromagnetic fluid
2. Magical loading of the astral body with the four divine fundamental qualities
3. Wish-realization through electromagnetic volts.

Magic Mental Training (IX) – Suggestions

Comment in Advance

Here is the same like in step VIII. It makes no real sense to create suggestions.

Magic Mirrors

"I work successfully with magic mirrors. I know all kinds of application. I know that I can use a magic mirror for clairvoyance, for the radiation of energies, as a transit gate to all desired planes and places, for communication with living and deceased persons, to get into contact with powers, beings, etc., for room impregnation, for purposes of influence, as a magic transmitter and receiver, for shielding and protection, for the projection of all the desired powers, pictures, paintings, etc. and to investigate the present, past and future. The more I use magic mirrors the easier it feels for me to work with them to reach my aims and to fulfill my tasks."

Magic Psychic Training (IX) – Suggestions

Astral Wandering

"Astral wandering feels as natural and easy as the mental wandering which I have mastered already. When I have left my physical body in my mental body, I can draw my astral body out by using my will power. The shape of my astral body is equal to the shape of my mental and physical body. Then I unite myself with my astral body by entering the astral shape. By conscious breathing in my astral body I connect my mental and astral bodies. By intensive training I become accustomed to breathing in my astral body. Only conscious breathing in the astral body is able to cause the separation of the astral matrix. When I begin breathing in my astral body, my physical body stops breathing. As the process of leaving the physical body is similar to death, feelings of fear can occur which I easily overcome by my will and confidence. I extend the distance from my physical body with every new exercise. I am able to cover greater and greater distances. The farther I move with my astral body from my physical body, its attractive power will become weaker and weaker. I know that I can travel the astral plane like the mental plane in the former exercises. The energy follows my will and intention and so I can bridge time and space easily with my astral body. I can visit all kinds of places in the astral realms and I can meet the living and the deceased ones. I can also create an astral place for my own purposes, my own astral temple or holy grove. The more I travel in my astral body the more I get used to it and the easier and natural it feels for me."

IMPREGNATION WITH THE FOUR DIVINE VIRTUES

"Thanks to deep meditations I am able to ecstasize directly with one of the four divine virtues, fusing with it in such a manner that I feel myself the virtue in question. I experience this ecstatic unity in the same with all four virtues of God. I can unite easily in great ecstasy with omnipotence, omniscience, wisdom, immortality and omnipresence. These great meditations are producing a kind of deification of my spirit and soul, and finally they influence my body in an analogous way, enabling me to establish the union with my God. From meditation to meditation it feels easier for me to unite with the divine virtues in real ecstasy."

Magic Physical Training (IX) – Suggestions

Talismans and Volts

"Thanks to my divine intuition I can charge and program all kinds of talismans, amulets and gems successfully. Thanks to my intense training and all the exercises it feels easy and natural for me to work with talismans, etc. for my aims and purposes. I can also charge electromagnetic volts easily and program them with my wishes."

Tenth Step - Suggestions

Summary of Exercises of Step X

Magic Mental Training:

1. Elevation of the spirit to higher levels.

Magic Psychic Training:

1. Conscious communication with the personal God.
2. Communication with deities, etc.

Magic Physical Training:

1. Several methods for acquiring magic faculties.

Magic mental training (X) – suggestions

The right attitude

"I bow in a spirit of great reverence in front of the Divine fount of Wisdom. There is no more pride or ambition nor superciliousness, to say nothing of bad qualities in his heart, for the deeper I penetrate into God's workshop, the more humble and receptive I become."

Visiting the realms of the elements

"With my mental body I can visit the different realms of the elements. I visit the kingdom of the gnomes, the kingdom of the nymphs, the kingdom of the fairies and finally that of the salamanders. For my visits I transform my mental body into one of the dwellers of the different realms. I charge myself mentally with the corresponding element and I take on the shape of a gnome, nymph, fairy or salamander. Then I go into the element realm and wait for the element beings to start contact. As soon as the dwellers of the element kingdoms begin to talk, they see in me a being higher in rank and superior to them and so they will make friends with me. When they are convinced about my superiority in willpower and intelligence, they will enjoy my company and become my most obedient servants and friends. In the kingdoms of the four elements I can learn everything about nature and creation, also about magical techniques for a diversity of purposes."

Meeting the spiritual guide

"Thanks to my mastership in mental wandering I am able to meet my spiritual guide face to face on the mental plane. I just have to express the wish to meet him and I will move immediately to him in my mental body. Face to face we can talk with each other like in a normal meeting with another person. First of all I will ask my genius when, how, and under what conditions I can contact him at any time. Certainly I will follow the instructions of my guide. Then I am ready to enter the last phase of my mental development, and as the physical world has nothing more to offer me, I will visit other spheres. According to the quabbalistic tree of life, I will reach in turns, first the sphere of the Moon, next the one of Mercury, then that of Venus, of the Sun, Mars, Jupiter and finally the sphere of Saturn. On all spheres I will meet the beings living there and I will learn to know all about their laws and secrets. When I have come so far my mental training is completed. I have become a perfect magician, I am a Brother of the Light, a true adept."

Magic psychic training (X) – suggestions

Uniting with God

"I am able to unite with God in all four manners successfully. I am a master in the mystical passive manner, the magic active manner, the concrete manner, and in the abstract manner. I know that the mystical and the magic way of uniting with God can be done in a concrete or abstract form. I can unite with divine virtues directly or I can use symbols, pictures or statues to embody the divine virtues. I can connect the divine virtues according to the elements with my different body regions. I connect the omnipotence with my head, divine wisdom with my chest, all-embracing love with my belly and immortality with my legs. I can also connect single virtues to single organs like love with the heart. My intuition guides me. The more I do the meditations about uniting with God and his virtues the more I refine myself and the more I integrate divinity in my personality. My meditations improve more and more so that I experience myself as

God, that I experience that there is nothing but God. "I am God!" or like Jesus said "The father and I are one!". The more I meditate about the unity with God and his virtues, the easier and natural it feels for me to become God, to embody God in my microcosm. I understand now that I am a temple of God."

COMMUNICATION WITH DEITIES

"Thanks to my intensive meditations I am able to unite with God and his divine virtues whenever I want. So I am well prepared to meet deities and high beings in the spheres not only as a magician but as a divine authority, as a god. As a divine authority I can communicate and work with other beings in a higher way. They show me respect and support my work as I represent the divine principle in creation. I have become a real ambassador of God."

MAGIC PHYSICAL TRAINING (X) – SUGGESTIONS

COMMENT IN ADVANCE

Suggestions for step X make only sense in a very limited range. Certainly you can focus on the development of special abilities as you like. Thanks to your mastership you have full access to all techniques, to abishekas, support of higher beings and the realization of all possible faculties.

Suggestion and telepathy

"I am a master of suggestion and telepathy. I can plant any kind of desired suggestion into the subconscious of a person for positive influences. I can receive and send thoughts. I can read the thoughts of others easily. I can communicate with people on the mental plane. I just have to shift my awareness consciously onto the mental plane and I have to perceive the other person in the same way, - as a mental being. Then we can connect for communication. My abilities of suggestion and telepathy increase daily and with every time I use them."

Psychometry

"I am a master of psychometry. I have the faculty to read the present time as well as the past and the future of any object. I am able to read the different events of the past, present or future with my mental eyes, ears or feelings. I just have to connect my mind to the object and then I perceive all things and happenings which are related to it. The more I train this ability the easier and natural it feels for me."

Additional Applications

The Right Attitude

Bardon describes the right attitude of the student respectively master. You can program yourself in this way.

"I am a student of the holy science and I know that only with the right attitude I will be able to reach mastership. And so from now on I am disciplined, diligent, patient and persistent in my training and my studies. Discipline, diligence, patience and persistence grow and develop in my personality and unfold completely. The spiritual world helps me to develop and strengthen these qualities in myself. From day to day I will grow in discipline, diligence, patience and persistence and so I will master all exercises and all challenges on my way to mastership."

"I love my spiritual training and I do my exercises with joy and enthusiasm. I love to do my training regularly so that it is anchored as a good habit and that it feels natural for me to do the exercises. I feel a natural need and desire to do my training always at the same time and at the same place as I know that this supports my progress and success in best way. The regular training gives me satisfaction and makes me feel good."

"As a true spiritual student of magic I know how important the refinement of the personality is. And so I behave in a friendly, tolerant and benevolent way. I do not condemn and I do not criticize others. I know that we all are not perfect, that we all make mistakes and regret bad behavior. My positive and kind attitude grows day by day and so it feels natural for me to act always in a friendly, tolerant and benevolent way. This feels good and I experience that my fellow men appreciate this kind behavior. It is good for all my relationships."

MEETING YOUR SPIRITUAL GUIDE

You can invite your spiritual guide for a meeting in the trance state – this means you meet him on the higher planes in your place, your temple or in a special, extra created room. You can ask him for inspiration, guidance, help, blessings or information. When your spiritual guide visits you, you will know it by his special radiation, - the atmosphere changes. Always be kind to your spiritual guide, ask him kindly for a meeting and thank him for coming and his gifts and say good bye to him at the end. In most cases your spiritual guide is so kind to come immediately. In some cases he is eventually too busy to come. Then try it on another day. In fact you can also ask deceased ones to visit you and many other beings. In all cases you should exactly know what you are doing and why. It is not something to play with.

"You are in your favorite place or temple and you want to meet your spiritual guide. It is time now to prepare yourself. Release all disharmonies of yourself and your place and create a holy atmosphere where your spiritual guide will feel well. Feel how the atmosphere becomes holy and now call your spiritual guide and kindly invite him to visit you now."

CLEARING AND HEALING

(This is one of the most important techniques which you can/should use once intensively and then from time to time. You can use instead of the white light also violet light. Very powerful is also a first round with violet light and then a second round with white light.)

"Imagine yourself sitting at a place you love to be, a place where you feel good and safe. Now imagine that suddenly the atmosphere around you becomes brighter and brighter. White light is gathering and it fills the atmosphere around you. More and more white light is coming from all directions and you feel that there is only you and the white light, you are sitting in the center of white brilliant light and you intuition says that this white light is something very special, a divine light as it radiates a great healing power, the power to clear and to heal everything which needs to be cleared and healed. And as you have this insight you feel how this white light enters your body from all sides. It enters your mental body, your mind, your subconsciousness. It enters your soul and your physical body. The white light fills your whole body, fills you completely on all planes, your whole microcosm, your aura, - all is filled with this white light and this white light is starting to work on you, to dissolve all your blockades and I mean all of them, all blockades in your energy channels, all blockades in your chakras, all blockades in your mind and in your soul and all blockades. The white light dissolves all blockades and it dissolves all negative thoughts and all negative emotions. The white light cleans you completely, your body, your energy system, your whole aura, your mind and soul. You receive a complete cleaning. And this feels simply great, absolutely great and you enjoy this cleaning process, this bath in white light. And more and more of this white light comes from all sides to enter your body, to clean you from all bad influences, from all blockades, from all negative thoughts and negative emotions, from all negative energies. And it feels really good to be clean, refreshed and balanced. And the white light unfolds its great healing power. It flows through your whole body, through your mind and soul, through all your organs and it heals you with great power, with great intensity and you realize that this cleaning and healing process is a gift of God for you as God wants you to be cleaned and healed, in full balance, in good health, vital and refreshed. And you feel more powerful and vital than ever before, you feel really great and you know that you master all challenges in your life with ease as God is with you and you are on the right path. There is nothing that could stop you. And you know what is right and necessary. You know the aims in your life. The white light cleans you, heals you, empowers you and also enlightens you. You are in the spirit of God, you are reconnected to the divine source of life, you are reintegrated into the natural-divine order and all what you need and wish for comes automatically into your life. And as you realize this you thank God in humbleness for his love and grace and whenever you need this divine light to clean and to heal you, to enlighten you then you can connect to it by a symbol, sign, gesture or word which comes now into your mind. (Short Break) Good. Keep this anchor in mind and work with it to reconnect to this power whenever you want or need it. Take some time to continue your bath in the white light, to clean and heal and to take part in the enlightenment. (Short Break) Good. You have enjoyed the white light and now it vanishes back into the universe where it came from. And you know that you can always connect with this white light whenever you want or need to, just by using your anchor, the sign, symbol or gesture which God has shown to you. And while the white light vanishes out of the atmosphere you rest a little bit more at the place you feel good and safe."

CLEARING AND HEALING OF OLD KARMA

(This is one of the most important techniques you can use for healing and for progress and the bettering of your life conditions. I highly recommend it! You can use it several times until you are absolutely sure that you are completely cleared and healed.)

"Imagine yourself sitting at a place you love to be, a place where you feel good and safe. Now imagine that suddenly the atmosphere around you becomes brighter and brighter. Violet light is gathering and it fills the atmosphere around you. More and more violet light is coming from all directions and you feel that there is only you and the violet light, you are sitting in the center of violet brilliant light and you intuition says that this violet light is something very special, a divine light as it radiates a great healing power, the power to clear and to heal everything of your former incarnations which needs to be cleared and healed. And as you have this insight you feel how this violet light enters your body from all sides. It enters your mental body, your mind, your subconsciousness. It enters your soul and your physical body. The violet light fills your whole body, fills you completely on all planes, your whole microcosm, your aura, - all is filled with this violet light and this violet light is starting to work on you, to dissolve all your karma blockades and I mean all of them, all blockades in your energy channels, all blockades in your chakras, all blockades in your mind and in your soul. The violet light dissolves your bad karma from all former lives and it heals all your wounds and all your injuries of your former incarnations. All these bad energies of mind and soul are completely released and cleared. You know that it is now the time to release all your bad karma and to heal all your wounds and injuries from all your former incarnations. Let your subconsciousness dissolve all these negative karma energies on all planes for a deep and complete healing. The violet light cleans you completely, your body, your energy system, your whole aura, your mind and soul. You receive a complete cleaning. And this feels simply great, absolutely great and you enjoy this cleaning process, this bath in violet light. And more and more of this violet light comes from all sides to enter your body, to clean you from all bad influences of your former incarnations, from all blockades, from all negative thoughts and negative emotions, from all negative energies of your past lives. And it feels really good to be clean, refreshed and balanced. And the violet light unfolds its great healing power. It flows through your whole body, through your mind and soul, through all your organs and it heals you with great power, with great intensity and you realize that this cleaning and healing process is a gift of God for you as God wants you to be cleaned and healed, in full balance, in good health, vital and refreshed. And you feel more powerful and vital than ever before, you feel really great and you know that you master all challenges in your life with ease as God is with you. Take some time to continue your bath in the violet light, to clean and to heal you from all of your bad karma, all injuries and wounds of your former incarnations. (Break) Good. You have enjoyed the violet light and now it vanishes back into the universe where it came from. And you know that you can always connect with this violet light of Akasha whenever you want or need to. And while the violet light vanishes out of the atmosphere you rest a little bit more at the place you feel good and safe."

PSYCHIC HYGIENE

"With every breath you go deeper and deeper in this wonderful state of trance and you listen to my voice and all I say anchors deeply in your subconsciousness. Imagine yourself taking a shower or a bath. Every time from now on whenever you take a shower or a bath you not only wash and clean your body but in fact you wash and clean your soul and mind from all negative thoughts, all negative emotions, from all stress and negative influences and bad energies. This happens automatically and naturally without the necessity to think about it. You wash and clean your mind and soul from all bad thoughts and bad emotions, from all stress and negative energies, every time you take a shower or a bath, completely automatically, completely naturally and this feels so good to be cleaned, to be fresh and healthy. Now imagine how you wash your hands. Every time from now on whenever you wash your hands, you not only wash and clean your physical hands but in fact you wash and clean your soul and mind from all negative thoughts, all negative emotions, from all stress and negative influences and bad energies. This happens automatically and naturally without the necessity to think about it. You wash and clean your mind and soul from all bad thoughts and bad emotions, from all stress and negative energies, every time you wash your hands, completely automatically, completely naturally and this feels so good to be cleaned, to be fresh and healthy. And every time whenever you go to the toilet you excrete also all bad emotions, all stress, all bad thoughts and all bad energies, so that these negative things are released and vanish down the drain automatically and naturally, without the need to think about it. And this feels really good for you. You feel pure, cleaned and balanced, really good. And every time from now on if something negative happens to you all your negative feelings and negative thoughts automatically drain off directly into the earth and the earth takes the bad energies from you and dissolves them. And you know that the earth is kind and does this to protect you and to keep you clean and in balance. And this happens naturally and automatically and there is no need to think about it. You feel thankful and happy that all bad energies are released from you to keep you in good mood, clean and fresh. And maybe you smile now how great this works and how easy it is for you to keep your balance and to feel clean and safe. And every time when you take a shower or a bath, every time you wash your hands and every time you feel upset or confronted with negative emotions then you experience that your mind and soul clean better and better and more and more effectively. And as you think about this great work of your subconsciousness you fall deeper and deeper into this wonderful state of trance. And you regenerate your mind, your soul and your body more and more. "

MASTERSHIP

"I want to tell you something about mastership. Real mastership means to have mastered both poles of a polarity. This means for example to master absolute power and at the same time total humbleness in the face of God. These are the two poles of one thing. Without total humbleness you will never gain total power and without the experience of total power you will never gain total humbleness. Both poles have to grow side by side, both have to be cultivated at the same time. And this is the key to mastership. It is the secret how two things are led back to the origin, to become one, to unite. And every time you feel in a way superior then you know that you have the necessary pole quality in yourself, - humbleness and might, love and power, wisdom and strength. And you know that you have to follow your own nature as God has foreseen it for every being. And when you are like a hawk then you cannot be a pigeon and when you are a lion or a tiger then you cannot be a sheep. This is the law of nature and you have to follow it. And so you have to reflect on yourself, on your true nature and not on any kind of images or what you think people expect from you. Be yourself and respect yourself, your true nature and follow what God has foreseen for you. Follow the will of God and unfold yourself. Become a real master and follow the path to perfection as it is meant for you. Master your life, enjoy your life, enjoy God and creation. Live a happy and fulfilled life. Do your training and unfold yourself. And when you show respect and understanding for the people you live and work with, then it is good and right and there is no need to hide yourself. You can be the one you are and you can follow your individual way as it is right, good and lawful. And from now on you are free of all blockades, - from now on you will follow your way as it is foreseen, good and lawful. From now on you will unfold your higher nature, yourself. And God will guide you by a refined intuition and you will know what is good and necessary for you."

IMMUNE SYSTEM

„Now I want to talk about the immune system. As you know a strong immune system is able to protect your physical health very well so that no disease is able to enter your body. A strong immune system keeps you healthy under all conditions and blocks all kinds of pathogens, blocks all diseases. From this day on you have a strong and healthy immune system which keeps your health and fends off all kinds of illness and diseases. And in the same way your physical immune system protects you and keeps your health, your psychic immune system will fend off all bad influences, all the stress, frustration and bad emotions from other people. From now on you will have a strong psychic immune system which keeps your mind and soul healthy, in good harmony, which will fight off all bad influences from other people, all bad emotions and all bad thoughts of others, so that you keep your inner peace and harmony, so that you keep a good emotional distance to bad behavior of other people. Indeed you cannot be contaminated by bad thoughts and bad emotions of other people any more. Your psychic immune system is from now on strong and protects your soul and mind from all bad influences and so you will keep your mental and psychic health, your inner peace and harmony in all challenges of life. And this is good to know and it gives you a feeling of immunity and self-confidence."

CHARISMA

"You have the desire to change something in your personality and life. You have a desire to increase and strengthen your positive characteristics and abilities. You want to improve your charisma, - the way you perceive yourself and the way other people perceive you. The charisma, the aura of a human being is very important as it determines our life. Everyone has an aura. Everyone has a specific, individual charisma and that is by which others measure and evaluate you. That is your way to impress and influence others. Charisma can have very different effects. Some people work with their charisma successful or powerful, while others act sensitively and sympathetically. Some look attractive while others seem trustworthy and reputable. People are called charismatic when their radiance is very strong and refined in a special aspect of their personality. They are people who have a very special influence on other people in a certain sense. And this with strong effects. Charisma can be controlled. It is malleable and changeable. With the help of your subconsciousness, you can set up your charisma as you want, as it is good and useful for you. Charisma is made up of a number of important factors that can be controlled consciously only with difficulty. The tone of voice, body posture, the process of movement, the expression of the eyes. The energy that surrounds a person, and even hardly detectable signals, such as the scent that the body emits using the finest fragrances have all a certain meaning. Similarly, the ideas and feelings which a human contains and cultivates have a strong effect on his charisma. His self-confidence, the inner peace or serenity, or the humor and the seriousness with which he approaches certain things. All this the Charisma shows. It helps its owner to achieve what he want to achieve, it helps him to be seen as he wants to be seen and it helps him to be successful in life, to be loved and accepted, to reach all aims and all this just by the use of his charisma. Imagine now a typical situation where the charisma you wish to have is missing. (Short Break)Very good, now please imagine, what would change in such a situation for you if you had the necessary, positive and strong charisma. How would the situation be like? (Short Break) Good and now imagine yourself in another situation where you unfold and use your positive charisma. (Short Break) Very good. And now take a third situation where you use your new and optimal charisma to reach your aims. Examine the impression you make on others and feel how easy life has become just by increasing your charisma. (Short Break) And now you anchor your new, positive, refined and strong charisma deeply in your subconsciousness as you wish it to be. Your imagination, your thoughts and feelings about the perfect charisma for you have helped your subconscious mind to understand what has to be done. And now your subconsciousness programs your charisma perfectly according to your wishes. And so all you want to communicate to others will be strengthened and intensified automatically, so that you will be understood well and your needs and wishes are supported. Your subconsciousness will adjust all the small details in a way that your charisma is intensive and in itself consistent. So that every movement, every word, every thought and feeling of you matches from day to day more and more with your wishes. And you will very quickly realize how my words come true, as I say it. All these words are deeply anchored in your subconsciousness and they are going to realize, as I have said."

SELF-RESPECT / SELF-CONFIDENCE

"You have the desire to do something for your self-confidence, your self-respect. Today you will make your wish come true. Self-confidence has many facets. It decides in many situations which behavior one chooses and is often critical to personal success. It can care for courage, for strength, for charisma and verve. The increasing of your self-confidence will help you to increase the whole quality of your life. You will gain new strength and you will increase your present abilities and powers even better. Maybe you'll be able to realize a few dreams which you haven´t reached so far. Please imagine a situation where you have lacked of self-confidence and how you have felt there. (Short Break) Very good, now please imagine what would change for you in such a situation with a good self-esteem, with a real good self-confidence. How does it feel like to have a good self-confidence? How do you experience such a situation? (Short Break) Very good. The fact, that you can imagine yourself with self-confidence in such situations is a first major step. Because it shows that you can realize it. Everything that you can imagine your subconscious mind is able to realize. Imagine that your subconsciousness begins to dissolve all the blockages which have kept you from feeling like you always wanted to. Your subconsciousness dissolves all your blockades now so that your self-esteem, your self-confidence unfolds and strengthens as it should be, as it is foreseen for you. It may be like a belt that is solved. Like a mist that dissolves. Feel how your subconsciousness dissolves all blockades in your personality and how new powers and qualities unfold for a healthy and strong self-confidence. It is a wonderful change which you witness. Maybe visions of a brighter future arise in your mind, situations where you master challenges with more confidence and with more inner strength, where you experience yourself as successful and happy. Maybe you feel some kind of tension when you think of mastering everything with real self-confidence und completely successful. Your subconscious mind realizes this process right now in you, it starts the positive changes. A metamorphosis. A development. And you will see how this development is realized bit by bit, step by step. You will feel how your self-confidence increases naturally and automatically from day to day. As it gets stronger and stronger you feel yourself more and more comfortable. You will feel how you become more and more the person you want to be. Because you can be it. This potential is in you, and from now on it is activated and will unfold itself completely. Your subconscious mind will help you with all its power, because it knows that you will feel better and better with this new unfolded self-confidence and therefore it is good for you, that it helps you. Imagine yourself in a few days or in a few weeks and how you radiate so much self-confidence. Imagine how it makes you smile and how great you feel with this. And imagine your posture. Imagine how upright and full of internal security you will go through life. Imagine how much pleasant feelings and moments of happiness you will experience by your unfolded self-confidence. Enjoy this process and look forward to all these major changes in your life.

You will be surprised how much energy and power is in you and how great life can be. All these words are in your subconsciousness deeply anchored and they are true, just like I said it. The change starts now and when you open your eyes again, then you may feel already that something is different, that something has already changed in you. And this feeling is becoming clearer and clearer until you have reached the optimal state that you wish to see."

THE RIVER OF LIFE

(This is very useful and recommendable to follow your individual sense of life in a natural, guided and successful way.)

"Please imagine now that the whole life is a long, cozy flowing river. It is a large, natural river maybe like the Amazonas or another big river you know. A river with long straight sections, but also with curves and turns. A river with wide, swiftly flowing points, but also with smaller areas and perhaps one or another sandbar. Imagine that you are sitting comfortably in a boat driving along the river. Imagine that you are sitting now here in this boat and that you just enjoy the trip. There is nothing for you to do - as the boat moves by itself, driven by the stream of the river and controlled by your subconscious mind, which works as an invisible helmsman who ensures that your boat stays on course. But sometimes in life it may be that the subconscious mind gets a little off course. Because it may not know which way to take when the river forks, or because it is too close to the shore where the stream is weaker and the boat loses momentum. Maybe sometimes it overlooks one or the other sandbank which makes the boat stuck for a while and sometimes it takes a long time, until the stream rises again and picks it up. Today I ask your subconsciousness to bring back your boat on the right course again in the natural stream in the middle of the river so that it can easily and fluently heading towards your goals. When your boat is on the right track, then the topics of life work out easily by flowing. Then life flows itself like this long, quiet river. Imagine how your boat moves more and more into the optimal position. Feel how it glides more and more easily and carefree. You can sit relaxed in it and just enjoy the trip. You can let yourself, your boat simply drift into the right direction and see how you drive naturally towards your aims in life, without being hindered by sandbars or driftwood. While you enjoy the relaxing trip, your inner helmsman is full awake. Your subconscious mind notices every curve, every sandbank well in advance and it leads your boat safely around them. Your subconscious mind will help you to find your optimal inner center and to reach your aims in a smart, fast and safe way. Your boat has reached the optimum driving position and keeps it from now on. And this makes you feel really good and relaxed as you know that your omniscient subconsciousness is the best helmsman for you in life. Your best guide in whom you can trust completely. Very well, your boat has now taken the right course and is ideal in the flow, in your inner center. In other words, your subconscious mind leads you exactly to your aims and uses the flow of life that gives the right energy to move forward. Sit back and enjoy the easy trip. 'Your subconscious mind will be always vigilant and taking good care of your course. It will control your boat all the time so that you stay centered within your inner self and make sure that nothing hinders you on your way. Just sit back and enjoy the easy trip."

MOTIVATION

You have the desire to improve your motivation. You have one or more goals in life that you want to reach and you feel that your drive, your activity is not strong enough to make it. That your inner power is not sufficient enough to reach fast enough or successful enough your goals. Hypnosis is a proven way to increase motivation, as it can activate all areas and powers inside of you which are necessary for full success and a high permanent motivation so that you will reach all your aims under perfect conditions. Motivation is needed for great things that you want to achieve as well as for necessities of everyday life. But mostly, it is needed for things that need extra energy or overcoming. Things which do not work out by themselves. A saying says that even the longest journey begins with a small step, and sometimes it takes many small steps and each one is important to get to your destination. Often one is confronted with doubts, fears and worries which hinders you on your path. It seems that you could not do it, that a force is missing, a lack of desire, something to address or sometimes quite a bit and normal human laziness. But in most cases it becomes easier with every step you make, is getting better and better completely automatic, all by itself. From now on your subconscious mind will mobilize all personal energies that are needed to motivate you, so that you work optimally for reaching your aims. Imagine a situation where you have lacked of the necessary motivation. What have you lacked? (Short Break) And now imagine this situation with full motivation. How does it feel for you? How has it changed? Isn´t it great to be full motivated and to reach your aims under best conditions? Imagine that from now on you have always the necessary motivation to reach all your aims with ease and satisfaction. Is that not appealing? You can have it all. Your subconscious mind supplies you with all you need for full success. It can organize everything in best way so that you work on your aims with full power and verve to reach your goals in best way. So that you go step by step your way and nothing is able to hinder you. An inner power will drive you step by step. And with every step of your journey it becomes easier and easier to follow you path to success. With each step you enjoy your work more and more. And with each step all your possible fears, doubts, uncertainties and worries vanish completely. Your desire and your ambition grow from day to day and nothing can hinder you from reaching your aims. All these words are anchored deeply in your subconsciousness. From day to day your strength, your ambition, your motivation are growing and you will feel a very significant change realizes in your life."

Superlearning

"Your subconsciousness will be set up now that you learn in the best way and that you can manage your knowledge perfectly. Your subconsciousness will be set up so that you absorb knowledge easily and whenever you want or need to recall and reproduce it, it will be easy and effortless too. From now on learning is quite easy for you, because your subconsciousness automatically activates all parts of your brain which are necessary for perfect learning whenever you want or need to learn. You will experience that learning is easy and fun for you. You will experience that from now on learning is quite simple and natural and that you feel motivated to learn effortless. Your subconsciousness set up your abilities in a way that knowledge enters your mind easily and that you can record this knowledge easily in your memory. Learning and reproducing of knowledge is quite easy, natural and makes fun. You remember things much easier and also learn whatever you want. – You will easily comprehend everything as your intuition guides you. Even the most complicated knowledge suddenly becomes very easy and understandable as your subconscious mind optimizes the work of your brain, of your mind and intellect. The whole process of perception, comprehension, memorizing and reproduction of knowledge is optimized by your subconsciousness. Everything works perfectly, naturally and automatically. And you enjoy this new way of learning. The knowledge that you absorb is so deeply stored in your memory that you can recall it easily at any time when you need it. Learning with the help of the subconscious mind is a great thing because it makes many things much simpler. The knowledge is naturally available. It's just there, if you need it. It is stored in a way that it shows up by itself whenever it is useful for you, whenever it is needed. From brain research we know that the brain gets into a very specific condition for optimal learning. It is a state of relaxed concentration. A state of relaxed attention. Optimal learning works very easy and effortless. And I want that your subconscious mind activates this special condition always then when you start to learn. All by itself, automatically, naturally. Your subconsciousness knows exactly how to set your brain activity in the right condition for perfect learning so that you learn very easy and that you can remember the subject matter perfectly. By experiencing this optimal learning condition your motivation to learn and the fun which learning brings will increase more and more. Learning is becomes suddenly something really nice. You no longer have to force yourself to learn but you will feel like a desire to learn coming naturally from inside. In most cases, learning is connected with an aim. For example with an exam or a test. Your inner being knows your aims and so your subconsciousness can set yourself perfectly for learning and the right preparation for tests and exams. It knows what knowledge you need and when you need it. And so you are always perfectly prepared for each test. Your motivation to learn increases automatically when you have to learn and so learning becomes easy and makes fun. And as it makes fun, the process of learning seems to be quite fast. The time flies. You are really motivated, you feel good and learning is exciting. Learning is from now on free of any stress, of any pressure. It just happens naturally. And as there is an optimum state for learning, there is also an optimum state for reproduction of knowledge. A relaxed concentration in which the knowledge is easily accessible. It is simply available, as it is needed. And also here your subconsciousness sets up everything as it is optimal for you. It makes your knowledge available. Easier and better than ever before. In tests you will notice that you are more relaxed than ever before and in the optimal condition and that the knowledge appears easily just in time as you need it. It will seem to you all questions and tasks are totally easy. Barely you have read or heard a question or task you immediately know the answer or know how to solve the problem in the right way. The answers come quickly and naturally. As if something inside of you would answer the question immediately, and the only thing which is left to do for you is to say the answer or to write it down. It may seem that in written examinations someone would just lead your pencil. Then you wonder now and then perhaps how automatically and perfectly it works. How simple it all is. You may even wonder how you can remember all that stuff. But that's normal, because it just works, as your subconscious mind supports you with all its power and this ability in you is in everyone and sometimes it just have to be activated as we do it now. In this way your performance will more and more improve. And you will learn easier and easier. Imagine this. Imagine how your life changes with this ability. Imagine what kind of chances, of opportunities open up for you. Imagine how useful this is, which advantages come along with perfect and easy learning, how great it is that your brain activates itself always for best learning and best reproduction of knowledge. How pleasant it is and how useful. From now on learning won´t be any more stress for you but indeed fun. Learning will be a very natural part of your life and will cost no effort any more as it simply works naturally and automatically. It will not affect your spare time any more. And from now on you will stop worrying about exams or preparing for it as you know that all works in a perfect and natural way. Now please imagine a situation where you experience this perfect and easy way of learning and reproducing knowledge. See yourself how you learn easily, how you comprehend and memorize knowledge. See yourself how easily you reproduce the learned stuff in a test, how easily the answers flow out of you, how your teacher is excited and happy about your perfect answers, about your perfect preparation. How does it feel for you? Isn´t it simply great and real fun?! Everyone is amazed about your fantastic skills in learning and memorizing and how naturally the answers come. How would you feel? What kind of opportunities would open for you? What would be better? What problems are then solved? Just imagine all of these points. How does it feel? (Short Break) All of these words and their effects, all your wishes and ideas are now deeply anchored in your subconsciousness and they will come true as it is good for you. You will feel that something has changed, as learning from now on is getting easier and your performance is getting better and better. Your subconscious mind will help you to express all your inner potential completely. It helps you to manage and organize your knowledge in such a way that you become more and more efficient and all your exam results are getting better and better. These words are deeply anchored in your subconsciousness and become true as I have said. And maybe you'll already feel how things change for the better. From now on you are perfectly set up to learn in an optimal way, to memorize perfectly and to reproduce your knowledge in best way, - naturally, automatically and effortless."

Epilogue

With this small book you have received a good, comprehensive package of suggestion for your autohypnosis exercises. Autohypnosis is in fact the master key to accomplish the steps of Bardon´s training. Without hypnosis and the work of the subconsciousness we use only 50% of our capacities. And when you calculate also your karma blockades then your performance is maybe only at 10-25%. So no wonder why many seekers have no real success.

When you use the information, instructions and suggestions of this book in an intelligent way then you will be amazed about the good results you gain and this with more natural ease in comparison to others.

I truly hope that this book serves many true spiritual seekers to unfold their divine nature. We need a lot of servants of the eternal light to master the challenges on earth.

I wish you the best for your spiritual journey!

In love, light and service,

Ray del Sole

Contact

Dear Reader,

if you like to contact me, please regard the following:

I can only provide answers for genuine spiritual seekers on the path – not for curiosity. Before you ask me try first to answer your question by own research as many questions of beginners and advanced students are already answered in my books and in the recommended spiritual literature.

Please respect that

- I have not much time for answering questions. I am very busy.
- I do not provide any magical help in any case. There are others who provide direct support.
- everyone has to go through the spiritual training by himself as training means a deep transformation of your personality, - there is simply no alternative. Discipline in training will let you reach all aims. Practice makes perfect!
- I am not interested in joining any kinds of circles, secret societies, brotherhoods etc.
- I am a genuine servant of the eternal light and only responsible to God, not to any kind of limited religion or human interests.

If you are interested in taking part in altruistic projects led by me in the future then you can mail me your name and email address and I will inform you when my projects start.

Please join my spiritual association: www.itf-sura.org

Please mail to: raydelsole@yahoo.de

Thank you for your understanding.

In love, light and service,

Ray del Sole

About the author:

I am an architect with special skills in management, eco-biology and economics. I have visited many foreign countries so that I got to know the beautiful diversity of cultures and people. I am a cosmopolitan and I feel at home especially in the south and the east of the world. I feel the old bonds of former incarnations to other countries, forms of old love and appreciation.

When I was a little child I have dedicated myself to the aim of understanding the world completely, how everything works. Today I would say – to understand God, man and creation, to gain real wisdom. So I started very early to study books about sciences, mysteries, religions, cultures, ancient history and spiritual teachings. Around the age of eighteen I began with the spiritual training system of Bardon. Indeed I chose this life to make as much spiritual progress as possible. And with this I will continue until I leave the material plane. For the future I have some spiritual, altruistic projects in mind. Let´s see what the coming years will bring.

Yours, Ray

INDEX

abilities 5, 19, 22, 23, 25, 27, 30, 34, 44, 46, 47, 48, 58, 60, 66, 74, 78, 80, 81, 88, 89, 98, 99, 104
Accumulation 52, 55, 58
air element 53, 63, 67, 75, 80, 81
Ajna Chakra 18
Akasha 27, 40, 55, 60, 63, 64, 65, 69, 78, 94
Akasha point 27, 64
amulets 85
anchor 29, 93, 99
asana 24, 27, 31, 50, 62
ASCETICISM 61
astral reality 33
ASTRAL SENSES 61, 71, 73, 74
Astral wandering 83
Auditory 44, 46
autohypnosis 16, 21, 22, 26, 28, 29, 30, 36, 48, 72, 107
automatic writing 66, 67, 68
autosuggestion 18, 21, 22, 29, 45, 48
Autosuggestion 21, 44
Back head chakra 18
bad karma 94
Bardon 1, 3, 14, 18, 19, 21, 22, 23, 29, 30, 37, 66, 67, 72, 81, 90, 107, 109
BEFORE SLEEP 51
Biomagnetism 52
Blessing of food 43
blockades 26, 27, 92, 94, 97, 100, 107
blood pressure 17, 22, 28, 35
Body control 45
BREAK 30

BREATHING OF THE ELEMENTS ... 53
Buddhism 31
chakras 19, 25, 26, 27, 92, 94
character 23, 31, 45, 48, 61
characteristics 34, 40, 41, 43, 48, 50, 98
charisma 56, 62, 98, 99
Choa Kok Sui 20
clairaudience 73, 75
clairfeeling 73, 80
clairvoyance 25, 73, 74, 82, 83
Clairvoyance 24
Concentration 39, 44, 45, 51, 52, 76
Conscious Breathing 38
Conscious pore breathing 45
Conscious pore-breathing 49
consciousness 18, 19, 21, 22, 25, 30, 35, 57, 58, 60, 64, 65, 70, 74
Contraindications 16
Control of thoughts 37, 38
CONTROL OF YOUR BODY 50
CONTROL OVER NEEDS 50
daring 52
Depression 16
Discipline of thoughts 37
earth element 53, 63, 80, 81
ecstasize 84
ecstasy 84
electric 76, 79, 80
element harmony 58
elementals 73
elementaries 74, 75
EMISSION OF ENERGY AT ONCE .. 56
Emptiness of mind 39
Eucharistic mystery 38, 42

EXTERIORIZING 68
fairies 86
fatigue 17
female pole 18, 19
fire element 53, 60, 63, 70, 80, 81
Fire element 18
first person perspective 31
flat 33, 77
fluid condensers 73, 76, 81
fluids 72, 76, 79, 80
four pillars 52
Full concentration 39
future 23, 24, 58, 78, 83, 89, 100, 108, 109
gems 85
gnomes 86
God 24, 40, 43, 84, 85, 86, 87, 88, 92, 94, 96, 108, 109
Hinduism 31
Hormonal disorders 17
house 33
hypnosis 16, 17, 21, 23, 35, 36, 48, 67, 107
hypnotherapist 28
hypnotherapy 23, 67
imagination 21, 23, 24, 25, 34, 37, 42, 43, 46, 47, 49, 52, 53, 54, 55, 56, 57, 59, 60, 64, 65, 67, 68, 70, 77, 79, 99
imbalance 19
immortality 84, 87
immune system 97
Impregnation of water 43
incarnations 3, 93, 109
induction 30, 33, 36, 69
injuries 94
inspiration 40, 73, 75, 91
intelligence 20, 70, 86

Introspection 37
intuition 27, 40, 41, 49, 50, 56, 57, 59, 61, 63, 72, 73, 75, 80, 81, 85, 87, 92, 93, 97, 104
Jesus 88
Jupiter 87
karma 61, 93, 94, 107
Knowledge 37, 52
lead out 30, 33
Lead out 35
LEVITATION 68
light 7, 24, 34, 53, 72, 74, 76, 79, 91, 93, 107, 108, 109
Low blood pressure 17
Magic Mental Training 37, 44, 51, 57, 63, 69, 73, 76, 82, 85
magic mirrors 76, 81, 82, 83
Magic of water 43
Magic of Water 38
Magic Physical Training 38, 45, 51, 58, 64, 69, 74, 76, 82, 85
Magic Psychic Training 37, 45, 51, 58, 63, 69, 73, 76, 82, 85
MAGICAL BALANCE 79
MAGICAL EQUILIBRIUM 61
magical training 25
magnetic 76, 79, 80
male pole 18, 19
Mars 87
martial arts 23
master 14, 23, 24, 41, 47, 49, 50, 55, 61, 65, 69, 70, 79, 87, 89, 90, 92, 94, 96, 100, 107
mastership 7, 23, 25, 52, 53, 56, 60, 61, 67, 71, 72, 79, 86, 88, 90, 96
maturity 30
meditation 22, 23, 24, 29, 31, 33, 34, 35, 48, 50, 67, 70, 74, 84

Mental wandering 77
Mercury 87
microcosm 20, 25, 26, 27, 52, 54, 61, 64, 65, 79, 88, 92, 94
Migraine 17
mind 14, 18, 19, 21, 22, 26, 27, 28, 29, 30, 31, 38, 39, 41, 42, 43, 44, 50, 51, 53, 55, 58, 60, 64, 70, 74, 77, 79, 89, 92, 93, 95, 97, 99, 100, 101, 103, 104, 109
Moon 87
motivation 70, 102, 105
MP3-file 29
mudra 31, 33
mystery of breathing 42
nature 24, 33, 34, 48, 59, 64, 65, 86, 96, 107
Neuro Programmer 3 29
nymphs 86
Observation of thoughts 38
Olfactory 44, 47
omnipotence 84, 87
omnipresence 84
omniscience 84
organs 20, 25, 55, 59, 60, 71, 79, 87, 92, 94
pain 17, 36
past lives 94
patterns 26, 48
pendulum 64, 68
Physical training 41
pika-pika-breathing 36
polarity 18, 19, 96
Pranic Healing 20
Process imagination 24
psychic hygiene 95
psychometry 80, 89
psychosis 16

quabbalistic tree of life 87
realms 24, 34, 69, 77, 84, 86
regression 23
relaxation .. 16, 21, 27, 31, 33, 36
religions 22, 109
repetition 21, 56, 59, 63
right attitude 15, 90
rituals 22, 29, 62, 63, 72
Rituals 58, 62
river of life 101
room impregnation 83
salamanders 86
Saturn 87
script 28
second person perspective 31
self-clearing 26, 27
self-confidence 19, 97, 98, 99
Self-criticism 37, 40
self-healing processes 26
self-knowledge 40, 41
Sensory 44
silence 52
simulation 23
solar plexus 63, 65
Solomon's 52
Soul refinement 48
Space impregnation 57
spiritual guide 20, 34, 64, 67, 68, 86, 91
stillness of mind 37, 39
Structure 25
subconsciousness 5, 14, 15, 18, 19, 21, 22, 24, 26, 27, 28, 29, 31, 33, 44, 46, 47, 48, 66, 67, 68, 81, 92, 93, 95, 98, 100, 101, 103, 104, 107
Subconsciousness 18
suggestions 16, 20, 21, 22, 28, 29, 30, 33, 37, 38, 40, 41, 45,

48, 49, 52, 53, 54, 58, 59, 61, 64, 65, 66, 70, 72, 73, 74, 77, 78, 81, 83, 85, 86, 87, 88, 107
Sun 87
Superlearning 104
talismans 85
Taste 44, 47
telepathy 89
telephone 28
Temperance 41
temple . 15, 33, 34, 52, 84, 88, 91
THE NOBLE MAGICIAN 78
THE RIGHT ATTITUDE 86
third eye 24
Thought control 37
throat chakra 25
traditions 22
trance 17, 21, 22, 27, 29, 30, 31, 32, 33, 34, 36, 65, 67, 68, 69, 91, 95

treatment 20
trigger 29
universe 53, 55, 58, 60, 61, 64, 65, 66, 93, 94
Venus 87
violet light 91, 93
Visual 44, 46
vital energy 49, 53, 54, 55, 56, 57, 59, 60, 62, 65, 72, 79
vital power 52
volition 52
volts 82, 85
waking state 17, 30, 33, 35
water element 53, 63, 70, 75, 80, 81
Water element 18
white light 91
wisdom 84, 87, 96, 109
worst case 30
wounds 27, 94

113

Made in the USA
San Bernardino, CA
29 November 2015